SO
BE
IT

Caroline Rothstein

LITERARY
ILLUSTRATION
CREATIVE
MEDIA GROUP

Copyright © 2022 Caroline Rothstein

All rights reserved. No part of this book may be reproduced
or used in any manner without the prior written permission of the copyright owner,
except for the use of brief quotations in a book review.

To request permissions, contact the publisher at info@licfiction.com

Paperback: 978-1-953046-20-8
Ebook: 978-1-953046-21-5

Library of Congress Number: 2020919301

First paperback edition March 2022.

Edited by Tialie Simpson
Book Cover Design by Dea Porcha Burch
Layout by Tialie Simpson and Dea Porcha Burch

Quotes from "A Time To Advance" by Chuck D. Pierce..

Printed by Color House Graphics in the USA.

Literary Illustrations Creative Media Group LLC
Detroit, MI 48204
licmediagroup.com

Scriptures marked KJV are taken from the KING JAMES VERSION (KJV): KING JAMES VERSION, public domain.

The names: THE NET BIBLE®, NEW ENGLISH TRANSLATION COPYRIGHT © 1996 BY BIBLICAL STUDIES PRESS, L.L.C. NET Bible® IS A REGISTERED TRADEMARK THE NET BIBLE® LOGO, SERVICE MARK COPYRIGHT © 1997 BY BIBLICAL STUDIES PRESS, L.L.C. ALL RIGHTS RESERVED

THE HOLY BIBLE, NEW INTERNATIONAL VERSION®, NIV® Copyright © 1973, 1978, 1984, 2011 by Biblica, Inc.™ Used by permission. All rights reserved worldwide.

Scripture quotations are taken from the Holy Bible, New Living Translation, copyright © 1996, 2004, 2007 by Tyndale House Foundation. Used by permission of Tyndale House Publishers, Inc., Carol Stream, IL 60188. All rights reserved.

"Scripture quotations are from The Holy Bible, English Standard Version® (ESV®), copyright © 2001 by Crossway, a publishing ministry of Good News Publishers. Used by permission. All rights reserved."

"Scripture quotations taken from the Amplified® Bible Classic, Copyright © 1954, 1958, 1962, 1964, 1965, 1987 by The Lockman Foundation Used by permission." (www.Lockman.org)

Table of Contents

DOUBLE PORTION — 9

JUDAH — 15

ISSACHAR — 23

ZEBULUN — 33

RUEBEN — 45

SIMEON — 53

GAD — 63

EPHRAIM — 71

MANASSEH — 79

BENJAMIN — 87

DAN — 93

ASHER — 101

NAPHTALI	**109**
PREPARE TO BATTLE	**115**
TRUMP	**125**
PRAYER	**129**

PREFACE

Judges 5:20 KJV

They fought from heaven; the stars in their courses fought against Sisera.

In August 2017, my husband planned a family trip to South Carolina to watch the eclipse. Two days before my family and I went to South Carolina, I was on the Internet, watching YouTube videos. I came across a guy who was praying for people who were firstborn children. He was praying for them to get back their birthright and their inheritance that the enemy has stolen.

John 10:10 (KJV)
10 The thief cometh not, but for to steal, and to kill, and to destroy: I am come that they might have life, and that they might have it more abundantly.

I found this interesting since my husband was the firstborn in his family. And it always seemed that he was the least favorite. His father and Stepmom had a beach house. We did not know each summer they would have a family reunion there but never invited us to any family reunion at the beach. However, his brothers and their families were, and his Stepmom's family was also. We were the only ones excluded from the annual family gathering.

The only reason I found out that they had family reunions every summer during the Fourth of July, at my in-laws' beach house, was because I was at work, and I was a charge nurse for the unit I worked on at the time. Another nurse came to me and shared that a patient frantically wanted to leave right then, but the doctor had not come to discharge her. I told her I would talk to her.

As I introduced myself and gave her my full name Caroline Rothstein, she, the patient, recognized me. It happened to be the Fourth of July week-

She says, "I know you. You're so and so's Rothstein's daughter-in-law. Why aren't you at the family reunion that you guys have every year at the beach house?"

They have not invited us to any of the family's reunions in over 20 years. I told her I did not know anything about it.

She says, "you guys have it every year."

Then she said she saw me and my kids' pictures on the wall when she was at their beach house. I thought back to what images that might be. Once I remembered, I explained that the photographs were not recent, and my children were very young then. My kids are grown up now. The look on her face revealed that she felt terrible for exposing the truth.

As I continued to watch this guy pray for people to regain their birthright, I thought it would be good to pray for my husband and see how God can restore my husband's firstborn birthright. That night, I laid in bed with my husband and prayed over him with the guy's prayers in the YouTube video. He referred to this scripture on the firstborn son.

Deuteronomy 21:17 KJV

17 But he shall acknowledge the son of the hated for the firstborn, by giving him a double portion of all that he hath: for he is the beginning of his strength; the right of the firstborn is his.

DOUBLE *Portion*

Deuteronomy 21:15 - 17 (KJV)

15 If a man have two wives, one beloved, and another hated, and they have born him children, both the beloved and the hated; and if the firstborn son be hers that was hated:

16 Then it shall be, when he maketh his sons to inherit that which he hath, that he may not make the son of the beloved firstborn before the son of the hated, which is indeed the firstborn:

17 But he shall acknowledge the son of the hated for the firstborn, by giving him a **double portion** of all that he hath: for he is the beginning of his strength; the right of the firstborn is his.

According to scripture, my husband should get a double portion; the man explained in the YouTube video. Because we believed the man's teaching, we prayed along with the YouTube video.

A couple of days later, we went down to South Carolina to watch the eclipse. For the first four days, we spent time at the beach in South Carolina before we went inland to watch the eclipse. The plan was to watch the eclipse in Easley, South Carolina. That first night, at the beach, I dreamt that my husband and I bought a house. I told him the next day, What I had dreamt. He said to me that would never happen; there is no way.

I was shocked because I always felt like these things were just too foolish for us, and I didn't think it was godly to have a place at the beach. But when I felt the Holy Spirit, Come up on me, I knew that this is what he wanted us to have. This was at the end of the summer season, So there is a lot of good deals. People wanted to sell because they don't make a lot of money during the winter seasons if they rent their property.

After seeing the eclipse, we went home. My husband and I decided to make an offer on the condominium. I knew God wanted us to have it. We gave an offer of $170,000. I feel like that that was the amount God wanted us to offer. The real estate person explained that they might feel offended by the offer, but I believe that number came from God. It was an excellent deal.

It turned out that our condo was on 77th St., and we bought it in the seventh month of the Hebrew calendar, Tishrei, which is during the months of September-October. Our condo number also is 714. Seven is the number of completion. I felt that somehow God was paying us back for the years that our family did not invite us to the family reunion. In December, we went back to visit our place. On Saturday, we went to a messianic congregation, and I told the Rabbi there our address. He right away said, "that's double the portion.". Suddenly, I remembered Praying the YouTube video and thought God is answering our prayers.

Later, I started to pray for getting back everything that the enemy has stolen from me and my family's bloodline. However, I did not seem to get any revelation or understanding of this prayer.

In spring 2019, I bought a book by Chuck Pierce called "A Time to Advance." This book is perfect for understanding the times and seasons. This book helps teach one to get optimal movement with God, to best reach their destiny. The book helps by understanding how to operate at specific times and seasons.

Ecclesiastes 3:2 KJV
A time to be born, and a time to die; a time to plant, and a time to pluck up that which is planted;

I bought the book, and after receiving it in the mail, I put it next to my bed. I had forgotten about it. About a month later, I had a dream, and I dreamt that I saw a man on a YouTube video saying a prayer, and he was mentioning different tribes of Israel by name in his prayer.

He said this is how you get everything stolen from your bloodline, on your mom's side and your dad's side. He mentioned each tribe of Israel. I thought this is very interesting and powerful; let me rewind the video. So I rewound it, and again he was naming off the different tribes of Israel in the prayer which I dreamt.

And he said, "again, if I had only known this prayer early, Life would've been so much easier."

I thought, wow, this is deep. I need to take notes on this, and I thought to myself, I'll have to come back to this and listen to it carefully. Then I woke up from my dream.

You only need ten tribes out of the twelve to receive your inheritance that the enemy had stolen throughout your bloodline. The number ten represents the "law" in correlation to the ten commandments. However, if we take a more in-depth look at the number ten, in Genesis 14:20, note: this is where Abraham paid Melchizedek ten percent of everything he owned. A tenth is also known as a tithe.

When God was going to destroy Sodom and Gomorrah, Abraham ended with the number ten. He asked God if there were ten righteous people there would you not destroy Sodom and Gomorrah, and God said if there are ten righteous people in Sodom and Gomorrah, he would not destroy it (Genesis 18:32).

With that said, I concluded it takes ten tribes of people to stand up to protect a territory from judgment. In addition, ten witnesses or tribes can assist in the divine council and convince the Father to overturn verdicts against us and convince God to rule in favor of us in the court of heaven to retore our birthrights. And this is perfect because I was going after what legally belonged to my family.

Starting to research the 12 tribes
I began studying the Bible about the 12 tribes. As I looked into all the blessings and what their names meant, Judah means praise. I knew Judah had to go first for my prayer because that was the order that they went into battle according to the Bible.

Judges 1:1-2 KJV
1 Now after the death of Joshua it came to pass, that the children of Israel asked the Lord, saying, Who shall go up for us against the Canaanites first, to fight against them?
2 And the Lord said Judah shall go up: behold, I have delivered the land into his hand.

And I found it interesting that when Israel went into battle, they would begin with praising God.

2 Chronicles 20:21-22 KJV
21 And when he had consulted with the people, he appointed singers unto the Lord, and that should praise the beauty of holiness, as they went out before the army, and to say, Praise the Lord; for his mercy endureth for ever.
22 And when they began to sing and to praise, the Lord set ambushments against the children of Ammon, Moab, and mount Seir, which were come against Judah; and they were smitten.

Also, when we get into God's presents before we begin to pray, we should give thanks, praise, and worship God. As indicated in **Psalm 100**:

1 Make a joyful noise unto the Lord, all ye lands.

2 Serve the Lord with gladness: come before his presence with singing.

3 Know ye that the Lord he is God: it is he that hath made us, and not we ourselves; we are his people and the sheep of his pasture.
4 Enter into his gates with thanksgiving, and his courts with praise: be thankful unto him and bless his name.
5 For the Lord is good; his mercy is everlasting; and his truth endureth to all generations.

If you are not a person who knows a lot about prayer, this is where you need to begin offering thanksgiving, praise, and worship unto the Lord.

I noticed two things as God gave instructions to the children of Israel to do as they moved into battle to take the promised land. One was the tribes' order as the children Israel entered the promised land. Two, they played the trumpet before they even went into battle.

Here is the order of moving in the camp. The men who blew the trumpets played first before the army.

Numbers 10:1-28 KJV
1 And the Lord spake unto Moses, saying,
2 Make thee two trumpets of silver; of a whole piece shalt thou make them: that thou mayest use them for the calling of the assembly, and for the journeying of the camps.
3 And when they shall blow with them, all the assembly shall assemble themselves to thee at the door of the tabernacle of the congregation.
4 And if they blow but with one trumpet, then the princes, which are heads of the thousands of Israel, shall gather themselves unto thee.
5 When ye blow an alarm, then the camps that lie on the east parts shall go forward.
6 When ye blow an alarm the second time, then the camps that lie on the south side shall take their journey: they shall blow an alarm for their journeys.
7 But when the congregation is to be gathered together, ye shall blow, but ye shall not sound an alarm.
8 And the sons of Aaron, the priests, shall blow with the trumpets; and they shall be to you for an ordinance forever throughout your generations.

9 And if ye go to war in your land against the enemy that oppresseth you, then ye shall blow an alarm with the trumpets; and ye shall be remembered before the Lord your God, and ye shall be saved from your enemies.

10 Also in the day of your gladness, and in your solemn days, and in the beginnings of your months, ye shall blow with the trumpets over your burnt offerings, and over the sacrifices of your peace offerings; that they may be to you for a memorial before your God: I am the Lord your God.

11 And it came to pass on the twentieth day of the second month, in the second year, that the cloud was taken up from off the tabernacle of the testimony.

12 And the children of Israel took their journeys out of the wilderness of Sinai; and the cloud rested in the wilderness of Paran.

13 And they first took their journey according to the commandment of the Lord by the hand of Moses.

14 In the first place went the standard of the camp of the children of Judah according to their armies: and over his host was Nahshon the son of Amminadab.

15 And over the host of the tribe of the children of Issachar was Nethaneel the son of Zuar.

16 And over the host of the tribe of the children of Zebulun was Eliab the son of Helon.

17 And the tabernacle was taken down; and the sons of Gershon and the sons of Merari set forward, bearing the tabernacle.

18 And the standard of the camp of Reuben set forward according to their armies: and over his host was Elizur the son of Shedeur.

19 And over the host of the tribe of the children of Simeon was Shelumiel the son of Zurishaddai.

20 And over the host of the tribe of the children of Gad was Eliasaph the son of Deuel.

21 And the Kohathites set forward, bearing the sanctuary: and the other did set up the tabernacle against they came.

22 And the standard of the camp of the children of Ephraim set forward according to their armies: and over his host was Elishama the son of Ammihud.

23 And over the host of the tribe of the children of Manasseh was Gamaliel the son of Pedahzur.

24 And over the host of the tribe of the children of Benjamin was Abidan the son of Gideoni.

25 And the standard of the camp of the children of Dan set forward, which was the rereward of all the camps throughout their hosts: and over his host was Ahiezer the son of Ammishaddai.

26 And over the host of the tribe of the children of Asher was Pagiel the son of Ocran.

27 And over the host of the tribe of the children of Naphtali was Ahira the son of Enan.

28 Thus were the journeyings of the children of Israel according to their armies, when they set forward.

Bingo!!! As mentioned above, this is the order that we must go into spiritual warfare to take back what the enemy has stolen from our entire bloodline.

Taking a closer look at verse 9, when Israel went into war, they had to blow the trumpets so that God would remember them and deliver them from their enemies. That pretty much guarantees success. God is a God of order. Putting it all together, let us look at verse 28, which talks about the tribes' journey into the promised land and the mandate God gave of the tribes on how to move in their journey. Amen!!! When we begin our journey to take back our "promised land," we will know how to proceed.

Remembering the dream when the man prayed, he kept mentioning individual names of the tribes of Israel. For example, he named Judah, Issachar, etc. I believe he was asking Israel's individual tribes to join him in the battle to get back everything that the enemy has stolen down his bloodline on his mom's side and dad's side.

As I researched the tribes of Israel, God gave me this revelation. After I had the dream and I kept searching about the 12 tribes of Israel. I could not figure out why the order was essential to God. How did the order come about? As I was praying for God to give me a revelation, all of a sudden, I reached beside my bed, and I picked up the book by Chuck D. Pierce titled *A Time to Advance*. I went right to the back, and I noticed the order that took place; it started with Judah, then Issachar Etc. It was in the same order as in The book of Numbers chapter 10. Bingo!!!

The tribal order is by the succession of the months in the Hebrew calendar starting with Nissan's month when Israel left Egypt (the month when Jesus died on the cross) and is not in birth order, chronological order.

We will look at each tribe, what each tribe of Israel represents, and their blessings and character. No doubt, when they were aligned and in right standing with God, they never lost a battle. The twelve tribes are like the body of Christ. We all work together using our gifts; some have skills and talents in some areas while others in other areas. However, when they all worked together with God, they are unstoppable.

TRIBE NAME

הַיְהוּדָ‎ה
Judah
or
Yehudah

HEBREW MONTH

נִיסָן
Nisan or Nissan
In the Torah it is called the month of the *Aviv*.
First month of the ecclesiastical year.

SYMBOL

STONE

EMERALD

SCRIPTURES

**Genesis 49:8-10
Deuteronomy 33:7
Genesis 29:35**

BIRTH MONTH

NISAN
(chodesh ha-aviv)

Occurs during the months of March-April.

Represents beginning of spring.

NAME MEANING

PRAISE

"Now will I praise the Lord."

SYMBOL

LION

the epitome of authority

STONE

Emerald

Intelligence and Wisdom

SCRIPTURES

Genesis 49:8-10
Deuteronomy 33:7
Genesis 29:35

BIRTH MONTH

NISAN-AVIV

NAME MEANING

PRAISE

SYMBOL

LION

STONE

EMERALD

SCRIPTURES

GENESIS 29:35
DEUTERONOMY 33:7
GENESIS 49:8-12

Caroline's COMMENTARY

Judah was born in the month of Nissan, the Jewish spiritual calendar's first month. The order does not go by chronological birth order, but by the first month. **Nisan** (or **Nissan**; **Hebrew**: נִיסָן, Standard **Nisan** Tiberian Nîsān) on the Assyrian **calendar** is the **first month** and the seventh **month** (eighth, in a leap year) of the Hebrew civil year. In the Tanakh, specifically the Book of Esther, it is referred to as **Nisan**. Let us look at some of the things that happen in the month of Nissan, Jesus rose from the dead, and Passover. This month represents redemption. It is around March/April.

Stone: Emerald

Symbol: Lion, symbolizes authority

Name Meaning: When Judah was born, Leah named Him.

Genesis 29:35 KJV
And she conceived again, and bare a son: and she said, Now will I praise the Lord: therefore she called his name Judah; and left bearing.

The most basic meaning of the word is **praise** or **worship**, but it means so much more.

The blessings of Judah
Israel spoke the first proclamation in Genesis over his sons, and Moses declared the second blessing in Deuteronomy.

Genesis 49:8-10 KJV
8 Judah, thou art he whom thy brethren shall praise: thy hand shall be in the neck of thine enemies; thy father's children shall bow down before thee.

9 Judah is a lion's whelp: from the prey, my son, thou art gone up: he stooped down, he couched as a lion, and as an old lion; who shall rouse him up?

10 The sceptre shall not depart from Judah, nor a lawgiver from between his feet, until Shiloh come; and unto him shall the gathering of the people be.

Deuteronomy 33:7 NIV
Hear, Lord, the cry of Judah; bring him to his people. With his own hands he defends his cause. Oh, be his help against his foes!

Final Thought:
Judah had a heart for his father, and he protected what concerned him. His father showed favoritism toward his sons that were born of Rachel, which were Joseph and Benjamin. Rachel was Jacob's true love. Joseph's brothers were jealous of him and wanted to kill him.

When Judah found out his brothers wanted to kill Joseph, he interceded and had Joseph suggested that they sell him to the Ishmaelites instead, and his brothers agreed. He protected Joseph from being murdered by his brothers (**Genesis 37:26-27**).

In **Genesis 44**, Because Judah thought Joseph was dead, he became even more protective of Benjamin Jacob's only known son left of Rachel. He knew that if he did not protect his only son left to him by Rachel, the heartbreak might kill his father. When Joseph hid a silver cup in

Benjamin's bag and later accused him of stealing it when they found it, Benjamin would now be sentenced to slavery. Judah stated, let me take his place.

Genesis 44:33-34 "Now then, please let your servant remain here as my lord's slave in place of the boy, and let the boy return with his brothers. How can I go back to my father if the boy is not with me? No! Do not let me see the misery that would come on my father."

Again, Judah was protecting what his father loved the most. No wonder why he blesses Judah with the scepter that would never depart. The tribe of Judah is represented by the lion. The Lion is the protector.

Caroline's Commentary

A king has a scepter, and it represents power and authority, so when we position ourselves with Judah we have the power and authority.

Hebrews 1:8 NIV
8 But about the Son he says,"Your throne, O God, will last for ever and ever; a scepter of justice will be the scepter of your kingdom.

Now, this is definitely who you would want to invite in you battle first, the tribe of Judah. Starting with praise and worship and restating his blessings

SCRIPTURES

Genesis 29:35 KJV

And she conceived again, and bare a son: and she said, Now will I praise the Lord: therefore she called his name Judah; and left bearing.

Genesis 49:8-10 KJV

8 Judah, thou art he whom thy brethren shall praise: thy hand shall be in the neck of thine enemies; thy father's children shall bow down before thee.

9 Judah is a lion's whelp: from the prey, my son, thou art gone up: he stooped down, he couched as a lion, and as an old lion; who shall rouse him up?

10 The sceptre shall not depart from Judah, nor a lawgiver from between his feet, until Shiloh come; and unto him shall the gathering of the people be.

Deuteronomy 33:7 NIV

Hear, Lord, the cry of Judah; bring him to his people. With his own hands he defends his cause. Oh, be his help against his foes!

ISSACHAR

ו

TRIBE NAME

יששכר
ISSACHAR
or
Yissaskar
northern kingdom

HEBREW MONTH

אייר
IYAR OR ZIV
Chodesh Haziv
Month of shining or blossoming.
Second month on the Jewish calendar.

SYMBOL

STONE

LAPIS LAZULI
or
Blue Sapphire

SCRIPTURES

**Genesis 49:14-15
Deuteronomy 33:18-19
1 Chronicles 12:32**

BIRTH MONTH

IYAR/ZIV
(Chodesh Ziv)

Occurs during the months of April-May.

A propitious time for healing

NAME MEANING

REWARD PAYMENT

"God hath given me my hire, because I have given my maiden to my husband".

SYMBOL

DONKEY

Strong burden bearer

STONE

LAPIS LAZULI
or
Blue Sapphire

SCRIPTURES

Genesis 30: 18
Numbers 10:15
Genesis 49:15
Deuteronomy 33:18-19
1 Chronicles 12:32

BIRTH MONTH
IYAR - ZIV

NAME MEANING
MAN OF HIRE, HE IS WAGES, THERE IS RECOMPENSE

SYMBOL
DONKEY

STONE
LAPIS LAZULI/BLUE SAPPHIRE

SCRIPTURES
GENESIS 29:35
GENESIS 49:8-12
DEUTERONOMY 33:7

ISSACHAR

ו

TRIBE NAME

יששכר
ISSACHAR
or
Yissaskar
northern kingdom

HEBREW MONTH

אייר
IYAR OR ZIV
Chodesh Haziv
Month of shining or blossoming.
Second month on the Jewish calendar.

SYMBOL

STONE

LAPIS LAZULI
or
Blue Sapphire

SCRIPTURES

**Genesis 49:14-15
Deuteronomy 33:18-19
1 Chronicles 12:32**

BIRTH MONTH

IYAR/ZIV
(Chodesh Ziv)

Occurs during the months of April-May.

A propitious time for healing

NAME MEANING

REWARD PAYMENT

"God hath given me my hire, because I have given my maiden to my husband".

SYMBOL

DONKEY

Strong burden bearer

STONE

LAPIS LAZULI

or

Blue Sapphire

SCRIPTURES

Genesis 30: 18
Numbers 10:15
Genesis 49:15
Deuteronomy 33:18-19
1 Chronicles 12:32

BIRTH MONTH

IYAR - ZIV

NAME MEANING

MAN OF HIRE, HE IS WAGES, THERE IS RECOMPENSE

SYMBOL

DONKEY

STONE

LAPIS LAZULI/BLUE SAPPHIRE

SCRIPTURES

GENESIS 29:35
GENESIS 49:8-12
DEUTERONOMY 33:7

Caroline's COMMENTARY

Issachar born in the second month which is **Iyar** also known as the month of **Ziv** which is around April/May. "The biblical name of **Ziv**, light, indicates that this month is a month for radiance and glory. **Iyar**, the acronym which reminds us that *"Hashem is our Healer."*

Stone: Lapis lazuli or blue sapphire

Symbol: Donkey, humility, faithful burden bearer, servant

Name meaning:
Genesis 30:18 KJV
And Leah said, God hath given me my hire, because I have given my maiden to my husband: and she called his name Issachar.

I like the meaning of Issachar from Wikipedia, Issachar meaning *reward*. **Issachar/Yissachar (Hebrew:** יִשָּׂשכָר, **Modern:** *Yissakhar*, **Tiberian:** *Yiśśāśḵār*, "reward; recompense") was, according to the Book of Exodus, a son of Jacob and Leah (the fifth son of Leah, and ninth son of Jacob), and the founder of the Israelite Tribe of Issachar. In another source it says perhaps "there is recompense", he will bring a reward;
Gifts, Abilities and Calling: Scripture says the tribe of Issachar had discernment of the times and the seasons. Mostly because of the amount of time they spend in deep study of the Torah.

1 Chronicles 12:32
KJV
32 And of the children of Issachar, which were men that had understanding of the times, to know what Israel ought to do...

NLT
From the tribe of Issachar, there were 200 leaders of the tribe with their relatives. All these men understood the signs of the times and knew the best course for Israel to take.

ESV

Of Issachar, men who had understanding of the times, to know what Israel ought to do, 200 chiefs, and all their kinsmen under their command.

NASB

Of the sons of Issachar, men who understood the times, with knowledge of what Israel should do, their chiefs were two hundred; and all their kinsmen were at their command.

NET

From Issachar there were 200 leaders and all their relatives at their command--they understood the times and knew what Israel should do.

The Blessings of Issachar

The blessings of Issachar were first spoken by Israel in *Genesis 49* and then again by Moses in *Deuteronomy 33*.

Genesis 49:14–15
KJV

14 Issachar is a strong ass couching down between two burdens:

15 And he saw that rest was good, and the land that it was pleasant; and bowed his shoulder to bear, and became a servant unto tribute.

NET

Issachar is a strong-boned donkey lying down between two saddlebags.

Deuteronomy 33:18-19 KJV

18 And of Zebulun he said, Rejoice, Zebulun, in thy going out; and, Issachar, in thy tents.

19 They shall call the people unto the mountain; there they shall offer sacrifices of righteousness: for they shall *suck of the abundance of the seas, and of treasures hid in the sand.*

Caroline's COMMENTARY

Notes: Issachar feast on the abundance of the sea, and on the treasures hidden in the sand. This tribe is without a doubt one to ask to join with you in your battle to reclaim all that was stolen from your bloodline. To feast on the abundance of the sea and to have the treasures hidden in the sand.

Mighty Warriors

Judges 5:15 KJV
"And the princes of Issachar *were* with Deborah; even Issachar, and also Barak: he was sent on foot into the valley. For the divisions of Reuben *there were* great thoughts of heart."

Here it talks about how the tribe of Issachar, was with Deborah and Barak in fighting against Sisera. Prophetess Deborah and General Barak knew how important it was to have Issachar with them, for Issachar understood whether or not it was a good time to go into battle.

Final Thought:

It is also particularly important to know when to go into battle and if the timing is right. Since the tribe of Issachar is known for its discernment times and seasons it is only right to have Issachar help us move in the right timing. We need to be sensitive to the Holy Spirit and ask the Lord is this the right time. With joining with Issachar, you might get the sense it is not the right time yet. You may have to take time to pray to seek when it is the correct time to proceed into battle.

Issachar crouches down, representing guarding the sheepfold, and is extraordinarily strong. He can handle a couple different burdens at the same time. This reminds me of myself.

Issachar also bowed his shoulder to bear burdens and became a servant. He helped with labor and worked hard. In my life for example, I am an ICU nurse and I have a family. God has graced me with the ability to handle the pressures of life yet manage the prayer burdens given to still go into battle for the things of God.

SCRIPTURES

Genesis 30:18 KJV
And Leah said, God hath given me my hire, because I have given my maiden to my husband: and she called his name Issachar.

1 Chronicles 12:32
KJV
And of the children of Issachar, which were men that had understanding of the times, to know what Israel ought to do...

NLT
From the tribe of Issachar, there were 200 leaders of the tribe with their relatives. All these men understood the signs of the times and knew the best course for Israel to take.

ESV
Of Issachar, men who had understanding of the times, to know what Israel ought to do, 200 chiefs, and all their kinsmen under their command.

NASB
Of the sons of Issachar, men who understood the times, with knowledge of what Israel should do, their chiefs were two hundred; and all their kinsmen were at their command.

NET
From Issachar there were 200 leaders and all their relatives at their command--they understood the times and knew what Israel should do.

Genesis 49:14–15 KJV
14 Issachar is a strong ass couching down between two burdens:

SCRIPTURES

15 And he saw that rest was good, and the land that it was pleasant; and bowed his shoulder to bear, and became a servant unto tribute.

NET
Issachar is a strong-boned donkey lying down between two saddlebags.

Deuteronomy 33:18-19 KJV
18 And of Zebulun he said, Rejoice, Zebulun, in thy going out; and, Issachar, in thy tents.

19 They shall call the people unto the mountain; there they shall offer sacrifices of righteousness: for they shall *suck of the abundance of the seas, and of treasures hid in the sand.*

Judges 5:15 KJV
"And the princes of Issachar *were* with Deborah; even Issachar, and also Barak: he was sent on foot into the valley. For the divisions of Reuben *there were* great thoughts of heart."

TRIBE NAME

ZEBULUN

זבולן

Gift or dowry

HEBREW MONTH

SIVAN

סיון
Chodesh Ha-Shlishi
Torah given at Mt. Sinai

SYMBOL

STONE

DIAMOND

SCRIPTURES

**Genesis 30:20
Genesis 49:13
Deuteronomy 33:18-19
1 Chronicles 12:33
Judges 5:14, 18**

BIRTH MONTH

SIVAN

סיון

May/June

Third month

Divinity

NAME MEANING

REWARD PAYMENT

"Now will my husband dwell with me",
Also means "man for hire."

SYMBOL

MERCHANT SHIP

STONE

DIAMOND

SCRIPTURES

Genesis 30:20
Genesis 49:13
Deuteronomy 33:18-19
1 Chronicles 12:33
Judges 5:14, 18
1 Chronicles 12:40

BIRTH MONTH
SIVAN

NAME MEANING
TO DWELL, GIFT, DOWRY

SYMBOL
MERCHANT SHIP

STONE
DIAMOND/CLEAR QUARTZ

SCRIPTURES
GENESIS 30:20 * GENESIS 49:13
DEUTERONOMY 33:18-19 * 1 CHRONICLES 12:33
JUDGES 5:14, 18 * 1 CHRONICLES 12:40

Carolines COMMENTARY

Zebulun was born in the third month of the Hebrew spiritual calendar in the month called Sivan, which is around May/June.

Stone: Diamond/Clear Quartz

Symbol: Ship (merchants in marketplace bring wares from different lands), commerce, business, wealth, trade.

Name meaning:

Genesis 30:20 KJV
And Leah said, God hath endued me with a good dowry; now will my husband dwell with me, because I have born him six sons: and she called his name Zebulun.

In the Old Testament **Zebulun** is the tenth son of Jacob (his sixth son by Leah) and the ancestor of one of the twelve tribes of Israel. As mentioned earlier in Genesis 30:20, it implies two different roots for the **name**: זָבַל (zaval) **meaning** "to dwell" and זֶבֶד (zeved) **meaning** "gift, dowry". Hence God had given Leah a dowry and her husband will dwell with her.

The blessings of Zebulun

The blessing first spoken over Zebulun was in Genesis 49 by Israel, and then in Deuteronomy 33 by Moses.

Genesis 49:13 KJV
Zebulun shall dwell at the haven of the sea; and he shall be for an haven of ships; and his border shall be unto Zidon.

Deuteronomy 33:18-19 NIV
18 About Zebulun he said: "Rejoice, Zebulun, in your going out, and you, Issachar, in your tents.

19 They will summon peoples to the mountain and there offer the sacrifices of the righteous; they will feast on the abundance of the seas, on the treasures hidden in the sand."

Notes: Zebulun and Issachar will feast on the abundance of the sea, and on the treasures hidden in the sand

1 Chronicles 12:33
KJV
Of Zebulun, such as went forth to battle, expert in war, with all instruments of war, fifty thousand, which could keep rank: *they were* not of double heart.

ISV
The tribe of Zebulun supplied 50,000 experienced troops, trained in the use of every kind of war weapon, in order to help David with undivided loyalty.

CSB
From Zebulun: 50,000 who could serve in the army, trained for battle with all kinds of weapons of war, with one purpose to help David.

Judges 5:14
KJV
Out of Ephraim was there a root of them against Amalek; after thee, Benjamin, among thy people; out of Machir came down governors, and out of Zebulun they that handle the pen of the writer.

They that handle the pen of the writer. Literally, *they who draw with the staff (shēbet) of the scribe (sophēr). Sophēr* may mean scribe (literally, "one who counts "), and the verb rendered "handle" is, literally, "draw;" but *shēbet* can hardly mean "pen"; nor is it easy to say of what special use "the pen of the writer" would be in the gathering of clans to battle; nor have we the faintest indication that Zebulun had any literary pre-eminence. There can be little doubt that the meaning is, "They who lead (so in Latin, *traho* sometimes has the meaning of *duco*) with the staff of the marshal."

Caroline's COMMENTARY

"The **sophēr** is the officer ... who musters, and therefore naturally counts and enrolls, the host ... and the staff: is his natural "rod of power," Commentary Ellicott's Commentary for English Readers

Judges 5:14
ESV
From Ephraim their root they marched down into the valley, following you, Benjamin, with your kinsmen; from Machir marched down the commanders, and from Zebulun those who bear the lieutenant's staff;

NLT
They came down from Ephraim— a land that once belonged to the Amalekites; they followed you, Benjamin, with your troops. From Makir the commanders marched down; from Zebulun came those who carry a commander's staff.

Judges 5:18
KJV
Zebulun and Naphtali were a people that jeoparded their lives unto the death in the high places of the field.

ESV
Zebulun is a people who risked their lives to the death; Naphtali, too, on the heights of the field.

NLT
But Zebulun risked his life, as did Naphtali, on the heights of the battlefield.

1 Chronicles 12:40 KJV
Moreover, they that were nigh them, even unto Issachar and Zebulun and Naphtali, brought bread on asses, and on camels, and on mules, and on oxen, and meat, meal, cakes of figs, and bunches of raisins, and wine, and oil, and oxen, and sheep abundantly: for there was joy in Israel.

ESV

And also their relatives, from as far as Issachar and Zebulun and Naphtali, came bringing food on donkeys and on camels and on mules and on oxen, abundant provisions of flour, cakes of figs, clusters of raisins, and wine and oil, oxen and sheep, for there was joy in Israel.

NLT

And people from as far away as Issachar, Zebulun, and Naphtali brought food on donkeys, camels, mules, and oxen. Vast supplies of flour, fig cakes, clusters of raisins, wine, olive oil, cattle, sheep, and goats were brought to the celebration. There was great joy throughout the land of Israel.

FINAL THOUGHT:

You want to also invite Zebulun into taking your cause of retrieving back everything that was stolen in your bloodline. After reading through the Scriptures and commentary, you can see the determination of the tribe of Zebulon in battle, as they risk their life as the scripture said. They also had the power of the pen. They are the ones that took note of who is fighting in the battle, and also engaged other tribes to join them. The pen could also represent a staff, representing authority. Scripture talks about that they will summon people to the mountains. They appear to be people that help gather people together for battle. They are people that feast on the abundance of the sea and have treasures hidden in the Sand. What a great reward there is through Zebulon

SCRIPTURES

Genesis 30:20 KJV
And Leah said, God hath endued me with a good dowry; now will my husband dwell with me, because I have born him six sons: and she called his name Zebulun.

Genesis 49:13 KJV
Zebulun shall dwell at the haven of the sea; and he shall be for an haven of ships; and his border shall be unto Zidon.

Deuteronomy 33:18-19 KJV
18 And of Zebulun he said, Rejoice, Zebulun, in thy going out; and, Issachar, in thy tents.

19 They shall call the people unto the mountain; there they shall offer sacrifices of righteousness: for they shall suck of the abundance of the seas, and of treasures hid in the sand.

1 Chronicles 12:33
KJV
Of Zebulun, such as went forth to battle, expert in war, with all instruments of war, fifty thousand, which could keep rank: they were not of double heart.

ISV
The tribe of Zebulun supplied 50,000 experienced troops, trained in the use of every kind of war weapon, in order to help David with undivided loyalty.

SCRIPTURES

CSB

From Zebulun: 50,000 who could serve in the army, trained for battle with all kinds of weapons of war, with one purpose to help David.

Judges 5:14
KJV

Out of Ephraim was there a root of them against Amalek; after thee, Benjamin, among thy people; out of Machir came down governors, and out of Zebulun they that handle the pen of the writer.

ESV

From Ephraim their root they marched down into the valley, following you, Benjamin, with your kinsmen; from Machir marched down the commanders, and from Zebulun those who bear the lieutenant's staff;

Judges 5:18
KJV

Zebulun and Naphtali were a people that jeoparded their lives unto the death in the high places of the field.

ESV

Zebulun is a people who risked their lives to the death; Naphtali, too, on the heights of the field.

1 Chronicles 12:40
KJV

Moreover they that were nigh them, even unto Issachar and Zebulun and Naphtali, brought bread on asses, and on camels, and on mules, and on oxen, and meat, meal, cakes of figs, and bunches of

SCRIPTURES

raisins, and wine, and oil, and oxen, and sheep abundantly: for there was joy in Israel.

NLT

And people from as far away as Issachar, Zebulun, and Naphtali brought food on donkeys, camels, mules, and oxen. Vast supplies of flour, fig cakes, clusters of raisins, wine, olive oil, cattle, sheep, and goats were brought to the celebration. There was great joy throughout the land of Israel.

TRIBE NAME

REUBEN
מחדש

Splendid son

HEBREW MONTH

TAMMUZ
תַמוּז
Fourth month

SYMBOL

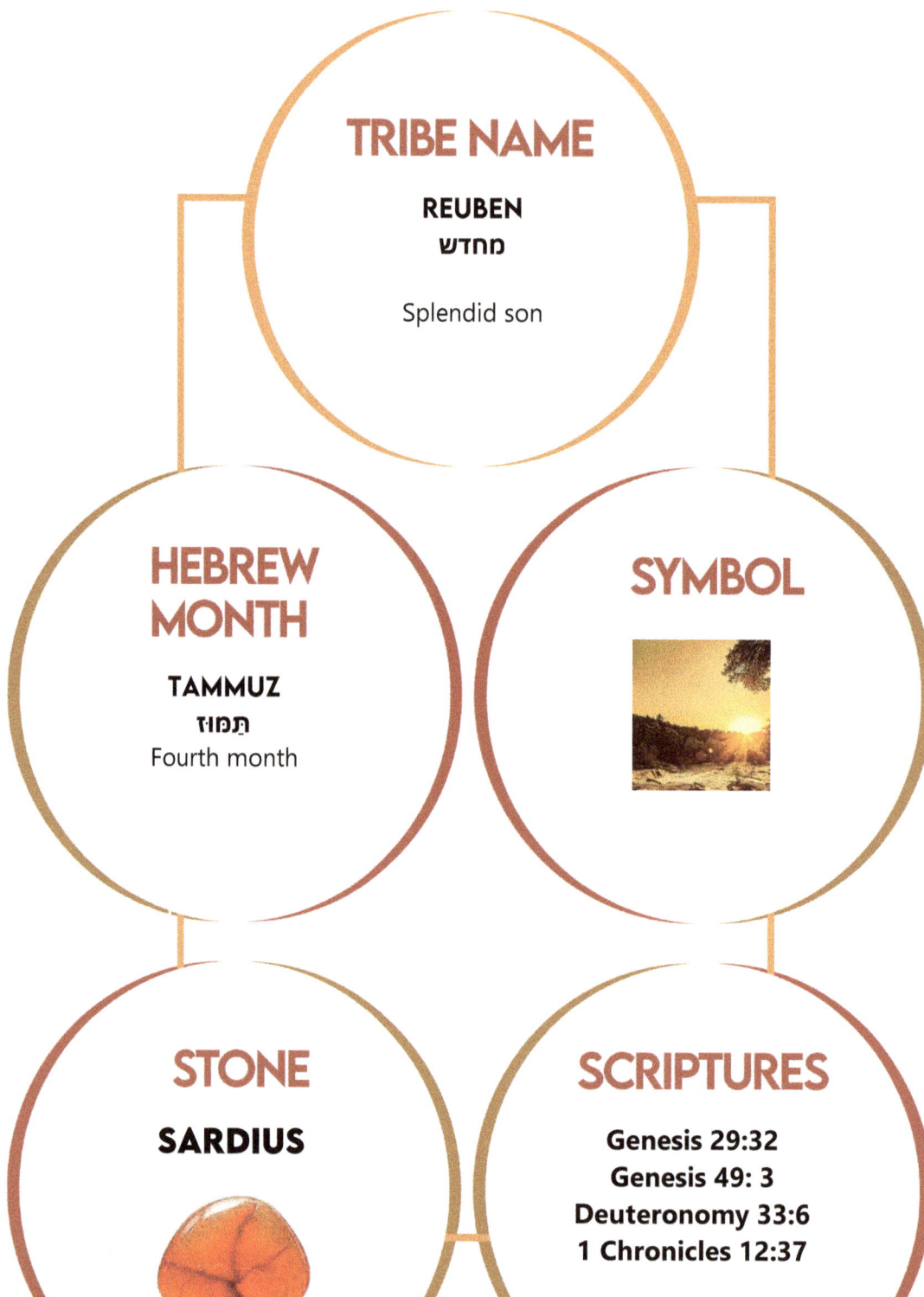

STONE

SARDIUS

SCRIPTURES

**Genesis 29:32
Genesis 49: 3
Deuteronomy 33:6
1 Chronicles 12:37**

BIRTH MONTH

TAMMUZ

תַּמּוּז

June/July

Fourth month

NAME MEANING

SPLENDID SON

'The LORD has noticed my misery, and now my husband will love me."

SYMBOL

RISING SUN

STONE

SARDIUS

SCRIPTURES

Genesis 29:32
Genesis 49: 3
Deuteronomy 33:6
1 Chronicles 12:37

BIRTH MONTH
TAMMUZ

NAME MEANING
BEHOLD THE SPLENDID SON

SYMBOL
RISING SUN

STONE
SARDIUS

SCRIPTURES
GENESIS 29:32 * GENESIS 49: 3
DEUTERONOMY 33:6 * 1 CHRONICLES 12:37

Carolines COMMENTARY

Reuben was born in the month of Tammuz, the fourth month, which coincides with June/July.

Stone: Sardius (reddish-orange)

Symbol: Rising Sun

Name meaning:
Genesis 29:32 KJV
"And Leah conceived, and bare a son, and she called his name Reuben: for she said, Surely the LORD hath looked upon my affliction; now therefore my husband will love me."

NLT
She named him Reuben, for she said, 'The LORD has noticed my misery, and now my husband will love me.

Reuben means "behold, a son" in Hebrew. In the Old Testament, he is the eldest son of Jacob and Leah and the ancestor of one of the twelve tribes of Israel.

The Blessings of Reuben

First spoken by Israel, Reuben's father proclaims over him in chapter 49 of Genesis. Then by Moses in Deuteronomy 33.

Genesis 49: 3-4 KJV
3 Reuben, thou art my firstborn, my might, and the beginning of my strength, the excellency of dignity, and the excellency of power:

4 Unstable as water, thou shalt not excel; because thou wentest up to thy father's bed; then defiledst thou it: he went up to my couch.

Caroline's Commentary

Deuteronomy 33:6 KJV

Let Reuben live, and not die; and let not his men be few.

1 Chronicles 12:37
KJV

And on the other side of Jordan, of the Reubenites, and the Gadites, and of the half tribe of Manasseh, with all manner of instruments of war for the battle, an hundred and twenty thousand.

CSB

From across the Jordan--from the Reubenites, Gadites, and half the tribe of Manasseh: 120,000 men equipped with all the military weapons of war.

Final Thought:

*I left out Reuben in my prayer because he slept with his father's concubine. In the above scripture of Genesis 49:4, Jacob pronounces a curse on Reuben, and because of it, it was my choice not to use him. However, if you feel the Holy Spirit leading you to keep him and remove somebody else, that should work also. The tribe of Reuben helped David against king Saul in the above scriptures.

SCRIPTURES

Genesis 29:32
KJV
"And Leah conceived, and bare a son, and she called his name Reuben: for she said, Surely the LORD hath looked upon my affliction; now therefore my husband will love me."

NLT
She named him Reuben, for she said, 'The LORD has noticed my misery, and now my husband will love me.

Genesis 49: 3-4 KJV
Reuben, thou art my firstborn, my might, and the beginning of my strength, the excellency of dignity, and the excellency of power:

4 Unstable as water, thou shalt not excel; because thou wentest up to thy father's bed; then defiledst thou it: he went up to my couch.

Deuteronomy 33:6 KJV
Let Reuben live, and not die; and let not his men be few.

TRIBE NAME

SIMEON

שִׁמְעוֹן

Hearer

HEBREW MONTH

AV

שֶׁל

Fifth month

SYMBOL

STONE

TOPAZ

SCRIPTURES

**Genesis 29:33
Genesis 49:5-7
1 Chronicles 12:25
Judges 1:1-3**

BIRTH MONTH

AV

July/August

Fifth month

NAME MEANING

HEARER

"Because Yahweh has heard that I was hated and he gave me this one also."

SYMBOL

WALLED CITY

STONE

TOPAZ

SCRIPTURES

Genesis 29:33
Genesis 49:5-7
1 Chronicles 12:25
Judges 1:1-3

BIRTH MONTH
AV

NAME MEANING
HEARER

SYMBOL
WALLED CITY

STONE
TOPAZ

SCRIPTURES
GENESIS 29:33 * GENESIS 49:5-7
1 CHRONICLES 12:25 * JUDGES 1:1-3

Carolines COMMENTARY

Simeon was born in the fifth month of Av, which is around July and August. The month of Av Is a very interesting month, a lot of catastrophic events take place on the ninth of Av. In the book Advance in Time by Chuck D. Pierce, on page 282 it lists tragic events:

1: Av 9 - 587 BC -The armies of Babylon destroyed Solomon's temple.

2: Av 9 - AD 70 - The Romans destroyed the 2nd temple

3: Av 9 - AD 135 - The final defeat of Jews by Roman.

The list goes on throughout history, but since this is not what this book is about, I will continue on with trying to get everything back that was stolen from us and our blood lines all the way back from Adam and Eve.

Stone: Topaz

Symbol: Picture of a Walled City, protection

Name meaning:
"In *Genesis 29:33* Leah, the wife of Jacob, says, "Because Yahweh has heard (shama) that I was hated and he gave me this one also" and she gives him the name שמעון (Shimon #8095), a Hebrew word meaning hearer."

Genesis 29:33 KJV
And she conceived again, and bare a son; and said, Because the Lord hath heard I was hated, he hath therefore given me this son also: and she called his name Simeon.

Genesis 49:5-7 KJV
5 Simeon and Levi are brethren; instruments of cruelty are in their habitations.

6 O my soul, come not thou into their secret; unto their assembly, mine honour, be not thou united: for in their anger they slew a man, and in their selfwill they digged down a wall.

7 Cursed be their anger, for it was fierce; and their wrath, for it was cruel: I will divide them in Jacob, and scatter them in Israel.

NIV

5 "Simeon and Levi are brothers—
   their swords are weapons of violence.
6 Let me not enter their council,
   let me not join their assembly,
for they have killed men in their anger
   and hamstrung oxen as they pleased.
7 Cursed be their anger, so fierce,
   and their fury, so cruel!
I will scatter them in Jacob
   and disperse them in Israel.

1 Chronicles 12:25
KJV
Of the children of Simeon, mighty men of valour for the war, seven thousand and one hundred
NKJV
Of the sons of Simeon, mighty men of valor fit for war, seven thousand one hundred;

Final Thought:
There were two instances in the Bible where Simeon's tribe was in trouble. The first time was in Genesis 49:5-7 where they were in the murder of a man. And the second was when the prince of Simeon brought back from the battle a temple prostitute which brought the anger of the Lord.

Carolines COMMENTARY

Which Phinehas stayed the Lord's anger and thus lifting the plague off of the camp of Israel when he killed the prince of Simeon and the foreign woman.

In Judges 1:1-3 Judah asked the tribe of Simeon to join them in battle and Simeon fought bravely and therefore had a part of the inheritance found in Judah. I chose not mention Simeon for spiritual warfare, to getting everything back in my bloodline, Because of the blessings he lacked a separated blessing apart from Judah. However, Simeon can be ruthless in battle against his enemies when needed.

1 Chronicles 12:25
KJV
Of the children of Simeon, mighty men of valour for the war, seven thousand and one hundred.

NLT
From the tribe of Simeon, there were 7,100 brave warriors.

SCRIPTURES

Genesis 29:33 KJV

And she conceived again, and bare a son; and said, Because the Lord hath heard I was hated, he hath therefore given me this son also: and she called his name Simeon.

Genesis 49:5-7

KJV

5 Simeon and Levi are brethren; instruments of cruelty are in their habitations.

6 O my soul, come not thou into their secret; unto their assembly, mine honour, be not thou united: for in their anger they slew a man, and in their selfwill they digged down a wall.

7 Cursed be their anger, for it was fierce; and their wrath, for it was cruel: I will divide them in Jacob, and scatter them in Israel.

NIV

5 "Simeon and Levi are brothers—
    their swords are weapons of violence.
6 Let me not enter their council,
    let me not join their assembly,
for they have killed men in their anger
    and hamstrung oxen as they pleased.
7 Cursed be their anger, so fierce,
    and their fury, so cruel!
I will scatter them in Jacob
and disperse them in Israel.

SCRIPTURES

1 Chronicles 12:25

KJV

Of the children of Simeon, mighty men of valour for the war, seven thousand and one hundred

NKJV

of the sons of Simeon, mighty men of valor fit for war, seven thousand one hundred;

1 Chronicles 12:25

KJV

Of the children of Simeon, mighty men of valour for the war, seven thousand and one hundred.

NLT

From the tribe of Simeon, there were 7,100 brave warriors.

TRIBE NAME

GAD
גאד

Fortune, luck
a troop cometh

HEBREW MONTH

ELUL
אֱלוּל

Sixth month

SYMBOL

STONE

AMETHYST

SCRIPTURES

Genesis 30: 10 - 11
Genesis 49:19
Deuteronomy 33:20-21
1 Chronicles 12:8-15
1 Chronicles 12:37

BIRTH MONTH

ELUL

אֱלוּל

August/ September

The six month

Bringing the harvest.

NAME MEANING

TROOP COMETH

"And Leah said, A troop cometh: and she called his name Gad. Also means fortune or luck.

SYMBOL

TENTS

STONE

AMETHYST

SCRIPTURES

Genesis 30: 10 - 11
Genesis 49:19
Deuteronomy 33:20-21
1 Chronicles 12:8-15
1 Chronicles 12:37

BIRTH MONTH
ELUL

NAME MEANING
GOOD FORTUNE

SYMBOL
TENTS

STONE
AMETHYST

SCRIPTURES
GENESIS 30: 10 - 11 * GENESIS 49:19
DEUTERONOMY 33:20-21 * 1 CHRONICLES 12:8-15
1 CHRONICLES 12:37

Caroline's COMMENTARY

Gad was born in the spiritual Hebrew month of Elul, who's also is around August/September. This is the month of bringing in the harvest.

Stone: Amethyst-Light Purple/violet

Symbol: Tents representing camp of soldiers (also found kid/goat, sheep, or dog)

Name meaning:
Genesis 30: 10 - 11
KJV
12 And Zilpah Leah's maid bare Jacob a son.

11 And Leah said, A troop cometh: and she called his name Gad.

NIV
10 Leah's servant Zilpah bore Jacob a son.

11 Then Leah said, "What good fortune!" So she named him Gad.

Means "fortune, luck" in Hebrew. In the Old Testament, **Gad** is the first son of Jacob by Leah's slave-girl Zilpah, and the ancestor of one of the twelve tribes of the Israelites. His **name** is **explained** in Genesis 30:11. Another **Gad** in the Old Testament is a prophet of King David.

The Blessings of Gad
Blessings spoken about Gad by Israel in Genesis 49 and Moses in *Deuteronomy 33*.

Genesis 49:19 KJV
Gad, a troop shall overcome him: but he shall overcome at the last.

Deuteronomy 33:20-21 KJV
20 And of Gad he said, Blessed be he that enlargeth Gad: he dwelleth as a lion, and teareth the arm with the crown of the head.
21 And he provided the first part for himself, because there, in a portion of the lawgiver, was he seated; and he came with the heads of the people, he executed the justice of the Lord, and his judgments with Israel.

1 Chronicles 12:37
[37] And on the other side of Jordan, of the Reubenites, and the Gadites, and of the half tribe of Manasseh, with all manner of instruments of war for the battle, an hundred and twenty thousand.

Final Thought:
Gad is another tribe you want to ask to join you in battle. He executes the justice of the Lord and his judgments with Israel.

SCRIPTURES

Genesis 30: 10 – 11 KJV
10 And Zilpah Leah's maid bare Jacob a son.
11 And Leah said, A troop cometh: and she called his name Gad.

NIV
Leah's servant Zilpah bore Jacob a son. ¹¹ Then Leah said, "What good fortune!" So she named him Gad.

Genesis 49:19 KJV
Gad, a troop shall overcome him: but he shall overcome at the last.

Deuteronomy 33:20-21 KJV
20 And of Gad he said, Blessed be he that enlargeth Gad: he dwelleth as a lion, and teareth the arm with the crown of the head.
21 And he provided the first part for himself, because there, in a portion of the lawgiver, was he seated; and he came with the heads of the people, he executed the justice of the Lord, and his judgments with Israel.

1 Chronicles 12:8-15 ESV
8 From the Gadites there went over to David at the stronghold in the wilderness mighty and experienced warriors, expert with shield and spear, whose faces were like the faces of lions and who were swift as gazelles upon the mountains
9 Ezer the chief, Obadiah second, Eliab third,
10 Mishmannah fourth, Jeremiah fifth,
11 Attai sixth, Eliel sevent
12 Johanan eighth, Elzabad ninth,
13 Jeremiah tenth, Machbannai eleventh.
14 These Gadites were officers of the army; the least was a match for a hundred men and the greatest for a thousand.
15 These are the men who crossed the Jordan in the first month, when it was overflowing all its banks, and put to flight all those in the valleys, to the east and to the west

1 Chronicles 12:37
37 And on the other side of Jordan, of the Reubenites, and the Gadites, and of the half tribe of Manasseh, with all manner of instruments of war for the battle, an hundred and twenty thousand.

EPHRAIM

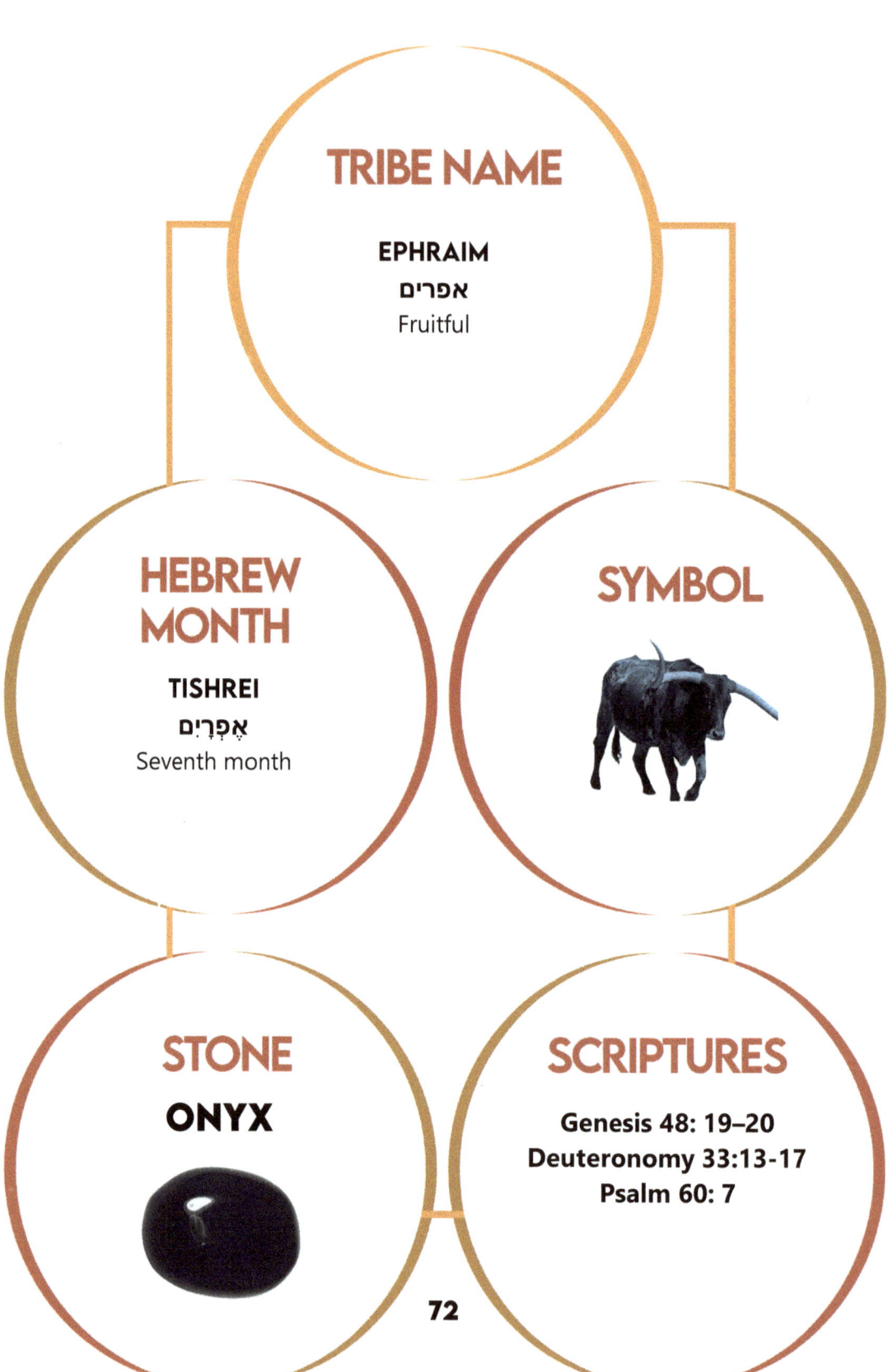

BIRTH MONTH

TISHREI

אֱלוּל

September/ October

The seventh month.

Month of Feasts

NAME MEANING

FRUITFUL

Son of Joseph and Asenath

SYMBOL

BULL

STONE

ONYX

SCRIPTURES

Genesis 48: 19–20
Deuteronomy 33:13-17
Psalm 60: 7

BIRTH MONTH
TISHREI

NAME MEANING
FRUITFUL

SYMBOL
BULL

STONE
ONYX

SCRIPTURES
GENESIS 48: 19–20
DEUTERONOMY 33:13-17
PSALM 60: 7

Carolines COMMENTARY

Ephraim born to Joseph in the land of Egypt. Joseph is not mentioned in the twelve tribes of Israel, especially when dividing up the land. Ephraim and Manasseh inherited their own territory of land. Throughout the whole Bible it mentions both Ephraim and Manasseh as tribes. For this reason, we will also keep them separate.

Ephraim was born in the seventh month of Tishrei. The number seven means completion. This month happens in the months of September/October. During this time, Israel has three Feasts: Rosh Hashanah, Yom Kippur, and Sukkot. This is a very powerful month in the Hebrew calendar.

Stone: Onyx

Symbol: Bull, symbolizes strength [bulls have horns, horns represent power, influence, strength]

Name meaning:
From the **Hebrew** name אֶפְרַיִם ('Efrayim) **meaning** "fruitful". In the Old Testament **Ephraim** is a son of Joseph and Asenath and the founder of one of the twelve tribes of Israel.

Other references of Ephraim in the Bible that is important to know:

Psalm 60: 7 KJV
Gilead is mine, and Manasseh is mine; Ephraim also is the strength of mine head; Judah is my lawgiver;

The Blessings of Ephraim

The blessings of Ephraim are stated by Israel in *Genesis 49:19-20* then added to by Moses in *Deuteronomy 33*.

Genesis 48: 19–20 KJV

19 And his father refused, and said, I know it, my son, I know it: he also shall become a people, and he also shall be great: but truly his younger brother shall be greater than he, and his seed shall become a multitude of nations.

20 And he blessed them that day, saying, In thee shall Israel bless, saying, God make thee as Ephraim and as Manasseh: and he set Ephraim before Manasseh.

Deuteronomy 33:13-17 KJV

13 And of Joseph he said, Blessed of the Lord be his land, for the precious things of heaven, for the dew, and for the deep that coucheth beneath,

14 And for the precious fruits brought forth by the sun, and for the precious things put forth by the moon,

15 And for the chief things of the ancient mountains, and for the precious things of the lasting hills,

16 And for the precious things of the earth and fulness thereof, and for the good will of him that dwelt in the bush: let the blessing come upon the head of Joseph, and upon the top of the head of him that was separated from his brethren.

17 His glory is like the firstling of his bullock, and his horns are like the horns of unicorns: with them he shall push the people together to the ends of the earth: and they are the ten thousands of Ephraim, and they are the thousands of Manasseh.

Caroline's Commentary

Final Thought:

Although they are both very great, according to the scripture Ephraim is greater than Manasseh. In Psalm 60:7 Ephraim is the strength of God's head and that is why he is the symbol of the bull, which has horns representing his power.

SCRIPTURES

Psalm 60: 7 KJV

Gilead is mine, and Manasseh is mine; Ephraim also is the strength of mine head; Judah is my lawgiver;

Genesis 48:19–20 KJV

19 And his father refused, and said, I know it, my son, I know it: he also shall become a people, and he also shall be great: but truly his younger brother shall be greater than he, and his seed shall become a multitude of nations.

20 And he blessed them that day, saying, In thee shall Israel bless, saying, God make thee as Ephraim and as Manasseh: and he set Ephraim before Manasseh.

Deuteronomy 33:13-17 KJV

13 And of Joseph he said, Blessed of the Lord be his land, for the precious things of heaven, for the dew, and for the deep that coucheth beneath,

14 And for the precious fruits brought forth by the sun, and for the precious things put forth by the moon,

15 And for the chief things of the ancient mountains, and for the precious things of the lasting hills,

16 And for the precious things of the earth and fulness thereof, and for the good will of him that dwelt in the bush: let the blessing come upon the head of Joseph, and upon the top of the head of him that was separated from his brethren.

17 His glory is like the firstling of his bullock, and his horns are like the horns of unicorns: with them he shall push the people together to the ends of the earth: and they are the ten thousands of Ephraim, and they are the thousands of Manasseh.

MANASSEH

נ

TRIBE NAME

MANASSEH
מנשה

Causing To Forget

HEBREW MONTH

CHESHVAN
חשוון

The eighth month

SYMBOL

STONE

JACINTH

SCRIPTURES

Genesis 41:51
Genesis 48: 19–20
Deuteronomy 33:13-17

BIRTH MONTH

CHESHVAN

חשון

October/ November

Eighth month. New Beginnings

NAME MEANING

CAUSING TO FORGET

First born son of Joseph.

SYMBOL

RE'EM

STONE

JACINTH

SCRIPTURES

**Genesis 41:51
Genesis 48: 19–20
Deuteronomy 33:13-17**

BIRTH MONTH
CHESHVAN

NAME MEANING
CAUSING TO FORGET

SYMBOL
RE'EM

STONE
JACINTH

SCRIPTURES
GENESIS 41:51
GENESIS 48: 19–20
DEUTERONOMY 33:13-17

Caroline's COMMENTARY

Manasseh the first born of Joseph. Born in the eighth month of Cheshvan which is also around October/November. The number eight spiritually represents new beginnings.

Stone: Jacinth

Symbol: Reem or Re'em or Reëm (unicorn, wild ox; not a horse), strength and steadfast, power [horn of the unicorn]

Name meaning:
Genesis 41:51 KJV
Joseph called the name of the firstborn Manasseh: "For God has made me forget all my toil and all my father's house."

Notice, the eighth months which is new beginnings, and the name Manasseh means *forget*. It's important when we start something new to forget what is behind us and to move into new territory, our new beginning.

The Blessings of Manasseh
The blessings of Manasseh, stated in like manner as all the other others were given one by Israel in Genesis 48 then another recounted in Deuteronomy 33 by Moses.

Genesis 48: 19–20 KJV
19 And his father refused, and said, I know it, my son, I know it: he also shall become a people, and he also shall be great: but truly his younger brother shall be greater than he, and his seed shall become a multitude of nations.

20 And he blessed them that day, saying, In thee shall Israel bless, saying, God make thee as Ephraim and as Manasseh: and he set Ephraim before Manasseh.

Deuteronomy 33:13-17 KJV

13 And of Joseph he said, Blessed of the Lord be his land, for the precious things of heaven, for the dew, and for the deep that coucheth beneath,

14 And for the precious fruits brought forth by the sun, and for the precious things put forth by the moon,

15 And for the chief things of the ancient mountains, and for the precious things of the lasting hills,

16 And for the precious things of the earth and fulness thereof, and for the good will of him that dwelt in the bush: let the blessing come upon the head of Joseph, and upon the top of the head of him that was separated from his brethren.

17 His glory is like the firstling of his bullock, and his horns are like the horns of unicorns: with them he shall push the people together to the ends of the earth: and they are the ten thousands of Ephraim, and they are the thousands of Manasseh.

FINAL THOUGHT:

As stated earlier, this is the eighth month which represents new beginning. Ephraim name means to forget so we forget what lies behind us and move forward.

SCRIPTURES

Genesis 41:51 KJV

51 Joseph called the name of the firstborn Manasseh: "For God has made me forget all my toil and all my father's house."

Genesis 48: 19–20 KJV

19 And his father refused, and said, I know it, my son, I know it: he also shall become a people, and he also shall be great: but truly his younger brother shall be greater than he, and his seed shall become a multitude of nations.

20 And he blessed them that day, saying, In thee shall Israel bless, saying, God make thee as Ephraim and as Manasseh: and he set Ephraim before Manasseh.

Deuteronomy 33:13-17 KJV

13 And of Joseph he said, Blessed of the Lord be his land, for the precious things of heaven, for the dew, and for the deep that coucheth beneath,

14 And for the precious fruits brought forth by the sun, and for the precious things put forth by the moon,

15 And for the chief things of the ancient mountains, and for the precious things of the lasting hills,

16 And for the precious things of the earth and fulness thereof, and for the good will of him that dwelt in the bush: let the blessing come upon the head of Joseph, and upon the top of the head of him that was separated from his brethren.

17 His glory is like the firstling of his bullock, and his horns are like the horns of unicorns: with them he shall push the people together to the ends of the earth: and they are the ten thousands of Ephraim, and they are the thousands of Manasseh.

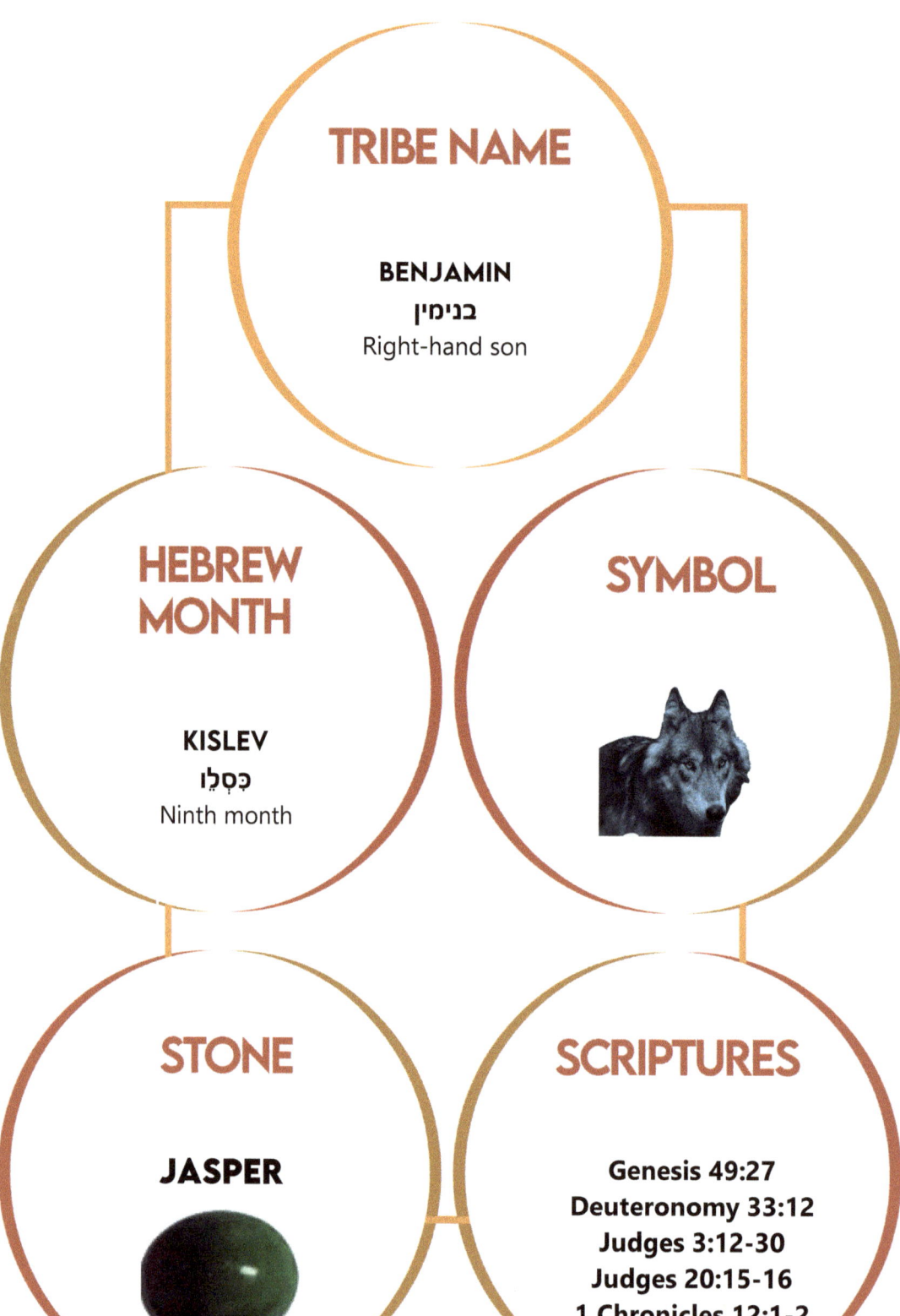

TRIBE NAME

BENJAMIN
בנימין
Right-hand son

HEBREW MONTH

KISLEV
כִּסְלֵו
Ninth month

SYMBOL

STONE

JASPER

SCRIPTURES

Genesis 49:27
Deuteronomy 33:12
Judges 3:12-30
Judges 20:15-16
1 Chronicles 12:1-2

BIRTH MONTH

KISLEV

כִּסְלֵו

November/ December

Ninth month

Sacrifice and Restoration!

NAME MEANING

SON OF THE SOUTH

Right-hand son or strong son.

SYMBOL

WOLF

STONE

JASPER

SCRIPTURES

Genesis 49:27
Deuteronomy 33:12
Judges 3:12-30
Judges 20:15-16
1 Chronicles 12:1-2

BIRTH MONTH
KISLEV

NAME MEANING
SON OF THE SOUTH

SYMBOL
WOLF

STONE
JASPER

SCRIPTURES

GENESIS 49:27 * DEUTERONOMY 33:12
JUDGES 3:12-30 * JUDGES 20:15-16
1 CHRONICLES 12:1-2

Carolines COMMENTARY

Benjamin was born in the ninth month Of Kislev which is also around the month of November/December.

Stone: Jasper (bright green)

Symbol: Wolf represents fierceness

Name Meaning:
From the Hebrew **name** בִּנְיָמִין (Binyamin) **meaning** "son of the south" or "son of the right hand", from the roots בֵּן (ben) **meaning** "son" and יָמִין (yamin) **meaning** "right hand, south".

The Blessings of Benjamin
The blessings spoken by Israel are in *Genesis 49:27*, and blessing spoken by Moses *Deuteronomy 33*.

Genesis 49:27 KJV
Benjamin shall ravin as a wolf: in the morning he shall devour the prey, and at night he shall divide the spoil.

Deuteronomy 33:12 KJV
And of Benjamin he said, The beloved of the Lord shall dwell in safety by him; and the Lord shall cover him all the day long, and he shall dwell between his shoulders.

Final Thought:
It is interesting to note that Benjamin was the only child born in the promise land. It is only appropriate to have him next because he is the start of the new beginning. Here is where we want to ask Benjamin to divide the spoils of our inheritance that was stolen from the enemy, And to dwell in safety and that the Lord cover us. In scripture we see that Benjamin received, five times the portion, of his brothers. Benjamin and Joseph had the same mother and father and therefore Joseph had a deep connection to Benjamin.

SCRIPTURES

Genesis 18:32-33

32 And he said, Oh let not the Lord be angry, and I will speak yet but this once: Peradventure **ten** shall be found there. And he said, I will not destroy it for ten's sake.

33 And the Lord went his way, as soon as he had left communing with Abraham: and Abraham returned unto his place.

Genesis 30:5-6

5 And Bilhah conceived, and bare Jacob a son.

6 And Rachel said, God hath judged me, and hath also heard my voice, and hath given me a son: therefore called she his name Dan.

Genesis 49:16–18 KJV

16 Dan shall judge his people, as one of the tribes of Israel.

17 Dan shall be a serpent by the way, an adder in the path, that biteth the horse heels, so that his rider shall fall backward.

18 I have waited for thy salvation, O Lord.

Deuteronomy 33:12 KJV

And of Benjamin he said, The beloved of the Lord shall dwell in safety by him; and the Lord shall cover him all the day long, and he shall dwell between his shoulders.

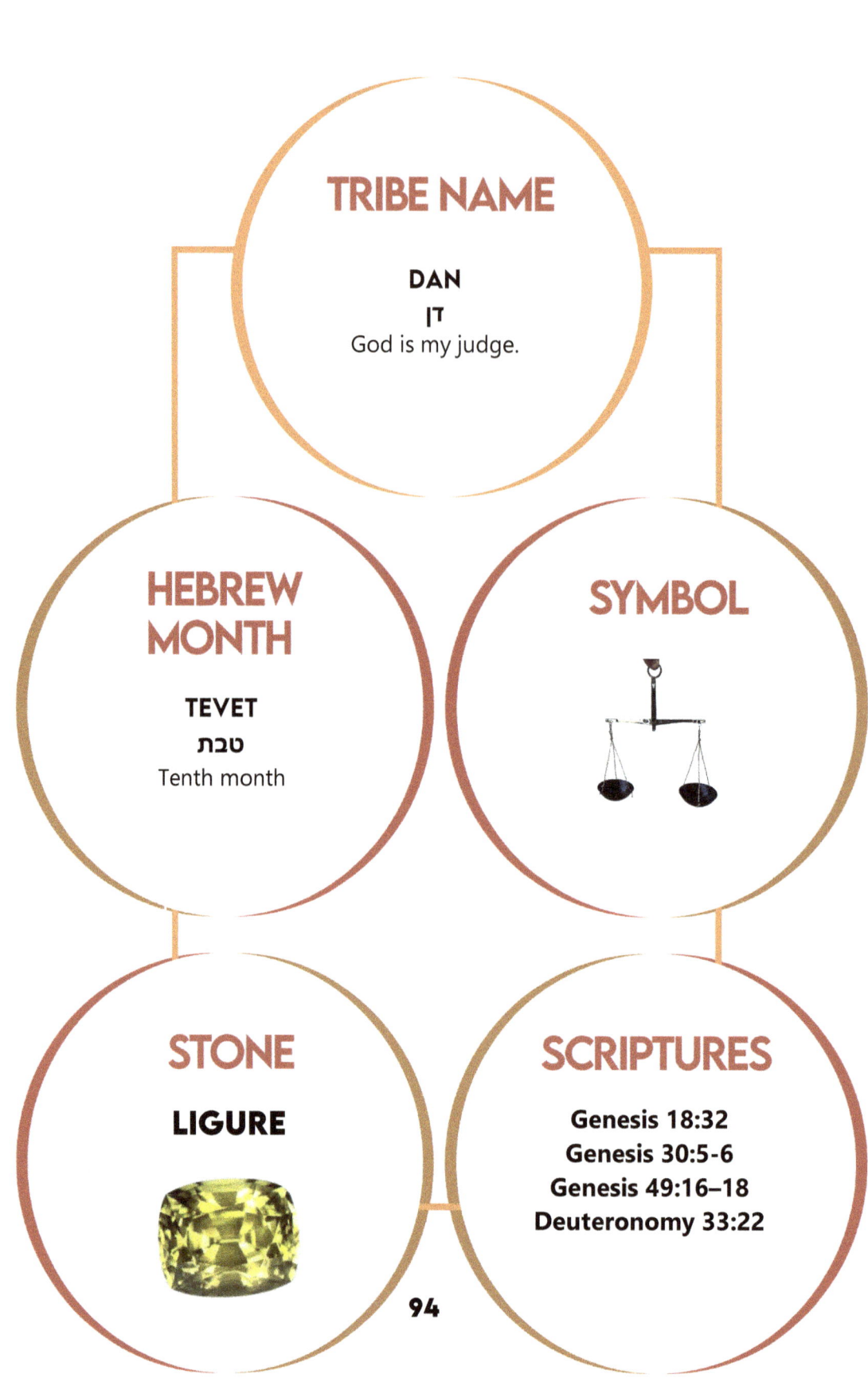

TRIBE NAME

DAN
דן
God is my judge.

HEBREW MONTH

TEVET
טבת
Tenth month

SYMBOL

STONE

LIGURE

SCRIPTURES

Genesis 18:32
Genesis 30:5-6
Genesis 49:16–18
Deuteronomy 33:22

BIRTH MONTH

TEVET

טבת

December/ January

The tenth month

Month of "Reflection."

NAME MEANING

GOD IS MY JUDGE

or
Govern

SYMBOL

PAIR OF SCALES

STONE

LIGURE

SCRIPTURES

Genesis 18:32
Genesis 30:5-6
Genesis 49:16–18
Deuteronomy 33:22

BIRTH MONTH
TEVET

NAME MEANING
GOD IS MY JUDGE

SYMBOL
PAIR OF SCALES

STONE
LIGURE

SCRIPTURES

GENESIS 18:32 * GENESIS 30:5-6
GENESIS 49:16–18
DEUTERONOMY 33:22

Caroline's COMMENTARY

Dan was born in the tenth Hebrew month of Tevet which is around December/January. When Moses was given the law from Jehovah there were ten commandments so there was a solid foundation. The number ten also represent government for example, when Abraham was talking with God about not destroying Sodom and Gomorrah God said he would not destroy it if there was ten righteous. It is inter-esting that Abraham stopped at the number ten.

Genesis 18:32 -33 KJV
32 And he said, Oh let not the Lord be angry, and I will speak yet but this once: Peradventure ten shall be found there. And he said, I will not destroy it for ten's sake.

33 And the Lord went his way, as soon as he had left communing with Abraham: and Abraham returned unto his place.

After looking at this, it is believed that if you have 10 righteous that they can change the course of action.

Stone: Ligure clear yellow stone

Symbol: Pair of scales, judgment and justice

Name meaning:
Dan, is Hebrew in origin, means "God is my judge".

Genesis 30:5-6 KJV
5 And Bilhah conceived, and bare Jacob a son.

6 And Rachel said, God hath judged me, and hath also heard my voice, and hath given me a son: therefore called she his name Dan.

The Blessings of Dan

Israel blessed Dan in *Genesis 49:16-18,* and Moses decreed blessings over the tribe of Dan in *Deuteronomy 33:22.*

Genesis 49:16–18 KJV

16 Dan shall judge his people, as one of the tribes of Israel.

17 Dan shall be a serpent by the way, an adder in the path, that biteth the horse heels, so that his rider shall fall backward.

18 I have waited for thy salvation, O Lord.

Deuteronomy 33:22 KJV

22 And of Dan he said, Dan is a lion's whelp: he shall leap from Bashan.

Final Thought:

Samson was from the tribe of Dan, and to this day, he is one of the most well-known judges in Israel and a great warrior. The story ended with Samson destroying the temple of Dagon. He pushed two middle pillars of the house down and destroyed the Philistines, which included all of their lords, in addition to men and women, which totaled around 3000 people.

(**Judges 16:23-30**). "**27** Now the house was full of men and women. All the lords of the Philistines were there, and on the roof there were about 3,000 men and women, who looked on while Samson entertained." ~***Judges 16:27 ESV***

This seems to be the evidence of the tribe of Dan living out their blessings; "Dan shall be a serpent by the way, an adder in the path, that biteth the horse heels, so that his rider shall fall backward." **Genesis 49:17**.

The adder is a 'horned serpent', that has the same color of sand and is not easily recognized. Here you have Samson being a prisoner and not being recognized as a warrior. The Philistines were deceived of who he truly was as a judge and a warrior.

Caroline's COMMENTARY

O Lord God, remember me, I pray thee, and strengthen me, I pray thee, only this once, O God, that I may be at once avenged of the Philistines for my two eyes."

After Samson judged the Philistines for what they had done to him, with his warrior spirit he was able to destroy them. The fact that he was disabled he did not appear to be a threat to the Philistines. The Philistines thought that he was no longer a warrior. Because of that, he was able to deceive them like a serpent.

This is where we want to ask for justice, for what was stolen from our bloodline from our family. We ask for the blessing of Dan to bring it forth.

SCRIPTURES

Genesis 30:5-6 KJV

5 And Bilhah conceived, and bare Jacob a son.

6 And Rachel said, God hath judged me, and hath also heard my voice, and hath given me a son: therefore called she his name Dan.

Genesis 49:16–18 KJV

16 Dan shall judge his people, as one of the tribes of Israel.

17 Dan shall be a serpent by the way, an adder in the path, that biteth the horse heels, so that his rider shall fall backward.

18 I have waited for thy salvation, O Lord.

Deuteronomy 33:22 KJV

22 And of Dan he said, Dan is a lion's whelp: he shall leap from Bashan.

TRIBE NAME

ASHER
אשר
Happy, blessed.

HEBREW MONTH

SHEVAT
שְׁבָט
Eleventh month

SYMBOL

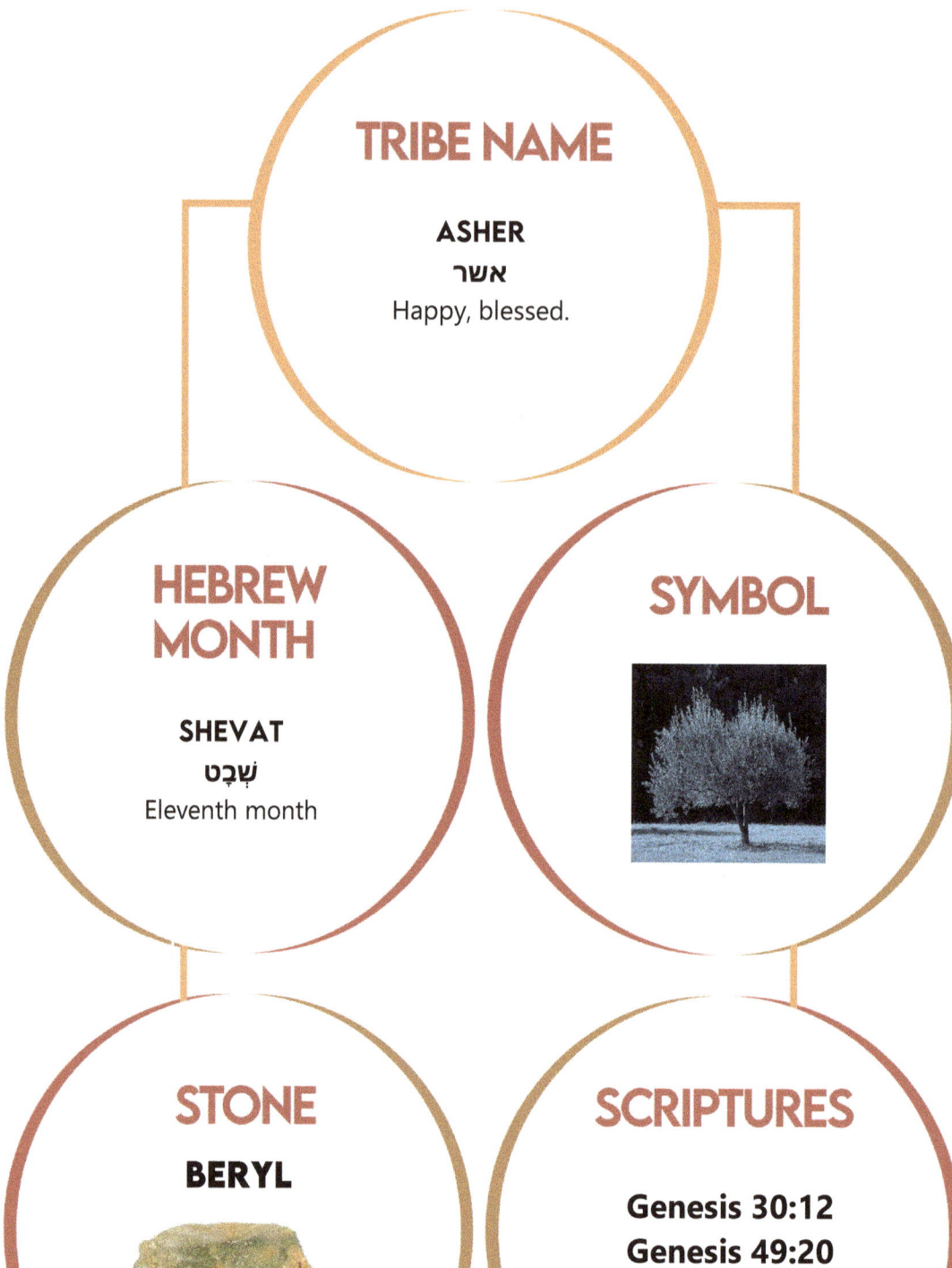

STONE

BERYL

SCRIPTURES

Genesis 30:12
Genesis 49:20
Deuteronomy 33:24

BIRTH MONTH

TEVET

שְׁבָט

January/ February

Eleventh month

"New year of the **trees**"

NAME MEANING

HAPPY, BLESSED

SYMBOL

OLIVE TREE

STONE

BERYL

SCRIPTURES

Genesis 30:12
Genesis 49:20
Deuteronomy 33:24

BIRTH MONTH
SHEVAT

NAME MEANING
HAPPY, BLESSED

SYMBOL
OLIVE TREE

STONE
BERYL

SCRIPTURES
GENESIS 30:13
GENESIS 49:20
DEUTERONOMY 33:24

Carolines
COMMENTARY

Asher was born in the eleventh month of Shevat of the spiritual calendar this is around the months of January/February.

Stone: Beryl (green to yellow)

Symbol: Olive tree, represents prosperity, beauty, and religious privilege

Name meaning:
Genesis 30:13 KJV
13 And Leah said, Happy am I, for the daughters will call me blessed: and she called his name Asher.

Asher's Jewish **name meaning** is "happy, blessed." I find it interesting he was born after Dan who brings forth justice. Once justice is done, we are very happy. It's time to praise God. we can receive these blessings, that were stolen from our bloodline.

The Blessings of Asher
Here are the blessings are spoken from Jacob in *Genesis 49:20* over his children and descendants. Moses also spoke blessings in *Deuteronomy 33:24*.

Genesis 49:20 KJV
Out of Asher his bread shall be fat, and he shall yield royal dainties.

Deuteronomy 33:24 KJV
And of Asher he said, Let Asher be blessed with children; let him be acceptable to his brethren, and let him dip his foot in oil.

Love to receive blessings of children (grandchildren etc.) Also, to be Acceptable to our brethren.

Final Thought:

God's is shown through the blessings of children (grandchildren etc.), and to be acceptable to our brethren. The dipping the foot in oil represent the foundational bloodline. Once justice is done, we are very happy. It's time to praise God, and we can receive these blessings, that were stolen from our bloodline.

SCRIPTURES

Genesis 30:13 KJV
13 And Leah said, Happy am I, for the daughters will call me blessed: and she called his name Asher.

Genesis 49:20 KJV
Out of Asher his bread shall be fat, and he shall yield royal dainties.

Deuteronomy 33:24 KJV
And of Asher he said, Let Asher be blessed with children; let him be acceptable to his brethren, and let him dip his foot in oil.

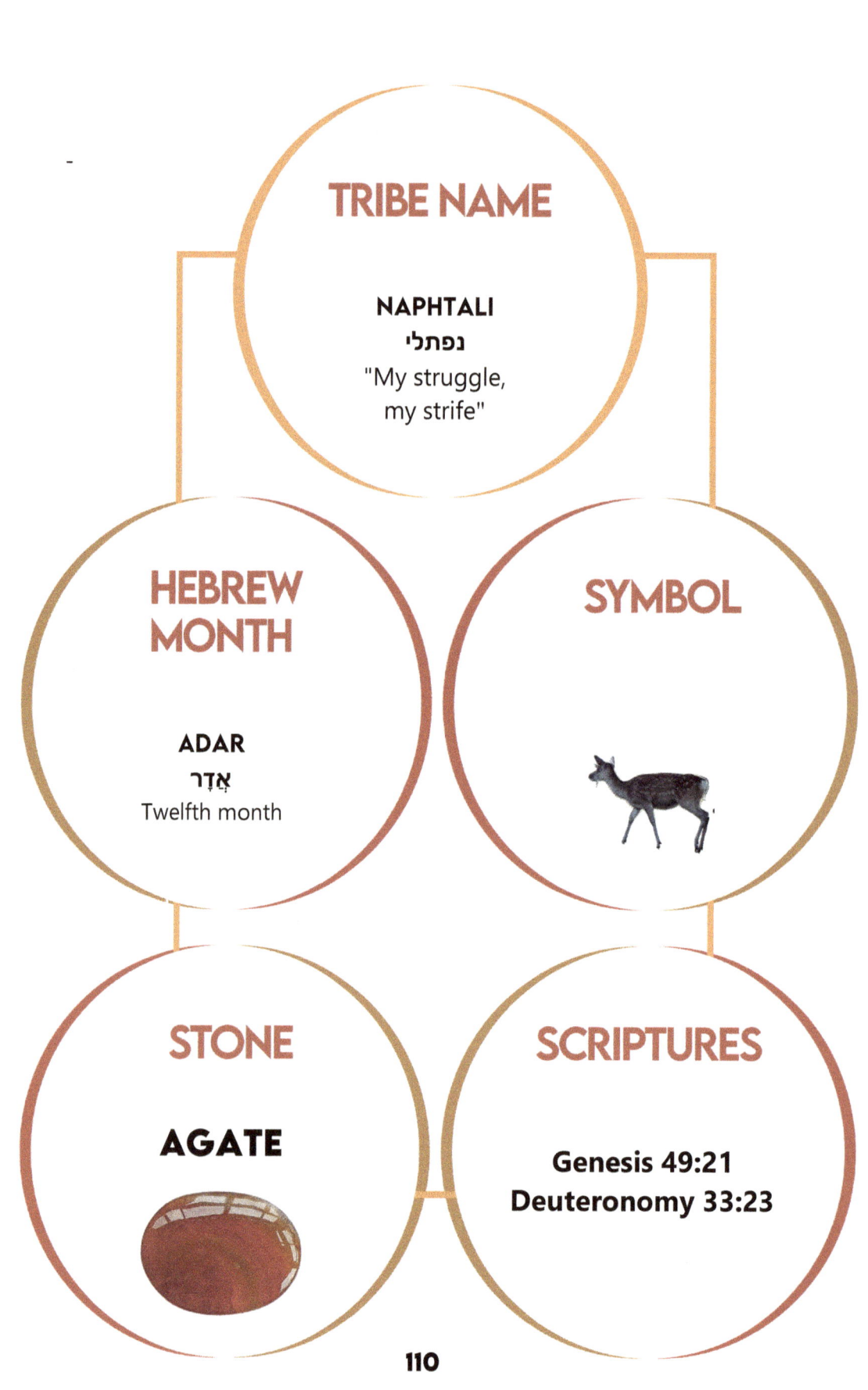

BIRTH MONTH

ADAR

אֲדָר

February/March
Eleventh month

"Time of the Purim Festival"

NAME MEANING

"MY STRUGGLE, MY STRIFE"

SYMBOL

DOE

(female deer)

STONE

AGATE

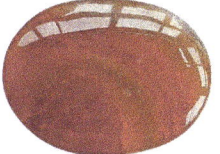

SCRIPTURES

Genesis 49:21
Deuteronomy 33:23

BIRTH MONTH
ADAR

NAME MEANING
"MY STRUGGLE, MY STRIFE"

SYMBOL
DOE

STONE
AGATE

SCRIPTURES
GENESIS 49:21
DEUTERONOMY 33:23

Caroline's COMMENTARY

Naphtali was born in the 12th month of Adar, which Is around the months of February/March. It is the time of Esther the story of Purim (celebration to commemorate victory of their enemies). Getting back with the enemy tried to steal.

Stone: Agate (Red/opague)

Symbol: Doe (female deer), swift and sure footing

Name meaning:
Genesis 30:8 KJV And Rachel said, with great wrestlings have I wrestled with my sister, and I have prevailed: and she called his name Naphtali

Naphtali means "my struggle, my strife" in Hebrew. In the Old Testament he is a son of Jacob by Rachel's servant Bilhah, and the ancestor of one of the twelve tribes of Israel.

The Blessings of Naphtali

The blessing spoken by Israel are in Genesis chapter 49:21 and spoken by Moses in Deuteronomy chapter 33:23.

Genesis 49:21 KJV
Naphtali is a hind let loose: he giveth goodly words.

Deuteronomy 33:23 KJV
And of Naphtali he said, O Naphtali, satisfied with favour, and full with the blessing of the LORD: possess thou the west and the south.

Yes, this is a perfect way to end a prayer with goodly words, giving thanks and praise and possessing all the blessings that were taken from are bloodline. We thank you Jesus and Jesus's name amen.

SCRIPTURES

Genesis 30:8 KJV

And Rachel said, with great wrestlings have I wrestled with my sister, and I have prevailed: and she called his name Naphtali

Genesis 49:21 KJV

Naphtali is a hind let loose: he giveth goodly words.

Deuteronomy 33:23 KJV

And of Naphtali he said, O Naphtali, satisfied with favour, and full with the blessing of the LORD: possess thou the west and the south.

PREPARE FOR BATTLE!

LAYING THE GROUNDWORK FOR BATTLE

Now we have an understanding of the 12 tribes of Israel. However, before we put it all together into a pray point, we need to self-examine ourselves. It is a spiritual battle. You must prepare before going into battle. Let us be clear that the battle on reclaiming our godly heritage that the enemy has stolen down our bloodlines. Suppose we look back at the story of Achan in Joshua chapter 7. He sinned, and it caused all of Israel to lose the battle at Ai. We do not want to lose the battle on a technicality. Remember, Satan is the accuser, and he has the advantage if we have unrepented sin. He can cause us to lose our battle.

Psalm 66:18 KJV
If I regard iniquity in my heart, the Lord will not hear me:

Isaiah 59: 2KJV
But your iniquities have separated between you and your God, and your sins have hid his face from you, that he will not hear.

John 9:31KJV
Now we know that God heareth not sinners: but if any man be a worshipper of God, and doeth his will, him he heareth.

REPENTANCE AND RENUNCIATIONS

Before we go into battle, we need to be positioned in the right relationship with God. We need to know who we are, that we are children of the most-high God Through the redemption of Jesus Christ of Nazareth, by his precious blood that was poured out and for the remission of our sins.

For most of my readers, you already made Jesus Lord and Savior. However, if you have not done so, this an opportunity to do so. The Bible says, "If you confess with your mouth that Jesus is Lord and believe in your heart that God has raised him up from the dead, you will be saved. **For, with the heart, we believe unto justice; but, with the mouth, confession is made unto salvation.**" Romans 10:9-10 **Douay-Rheims Bible** (Romans 8:9) Simply stated, "Jesus is my Lord and Savior. I confess my sins." Now you are a part of the kingdom of God.

The next thing we need to do is repent. It all begins with the motives of the heart. The heart and the mind are connected. When it first enters our hearts, we think about what we are going to do. We might ponder in our hearts what we are going to say and doing. That is why we have to guard our hearts (Matthew 5:28).

Matthew 5:28 KJV

28 But I say unto you, That whosoever looketh on a woman to lust after her hath committed adultery with her already in his heart.

Repenting means turning away from the sin first in your mindset and then determining to change your actions from the former way of thinking and doing. And renouncing means that the sin no longer recognizes you. The best way of repenting and renouncing our sin is to take scripture and use it, for example:

Galatians 5:19-21 NKJV

19 Now the works of the flesh are evident, which are: [a]adultery, [b]fornication, uncleanness, lewdness,

20 idolatry, sorcery, hatred, contentions, jealousies, outbursts of wrath, selfish ambitions, dissensions, heresies,

21 envy, [c]murders, drunkenness, revelries, and the like; of which I tell you beforehand, just as I also told you in time past, that those who practice such things will not inherit the kingdom of God.

*Here is an example below of how to use the above scripture and turn it into repentance as well as a renunciation.

I repent of adultery, (confess anytime of adulterous thoughts, deeds, actions, relationship), and renounce adultery, I am not an adulterer.

I repent of fornication, (confess anytime of fornicating), and renounce fornication, I am not a fornicator.

I repent of uncleanliness, I renounce all forms of uncleanness (confess anytime of being unclean), and I am no longer unclean.

I repent of lewdness, (confess anytime of being lewd), and renounce lewdness, I am not lewd.

I repent of idolatry, (confess any situation of idolatry), and I am not an idolater.

I repent of sorcery (confess anytime of doing sorcery such as: witchcraft, ouija board, séances, palm reading, fortunetelling, occult practices etc.), and renounce I am not a sorcery.

I repent of causing contention, (confess anytime of causing contention), and renounce, I am not a person of contention.

I repent of being jealous, (then confess any situation you know you've had a feeling of jealousy), and renounce I am not a jealous person.

I repent of outburst of wrath, (confess anytime of outburst of wrath), and renounce I am not a person who has outburst of wrath.

I repent of selfish ambition, (confess of any situation of selfish ambition), and renounce, I am not a person who pursue selfish ambitions.

I repent of dissensions, (confess of any situation of causing dissensions), and renounce I am not a person who causes dissension.

I repent of heresies, (confess of any heresies in your life), and renounce, I am not a heretic.

I repent of envy, (confess of any situation of envy), and renounce, I am not envious.

I repent of murder, (confess anytime you had murdered somebody), and renounce, I am not a murderer.

I repent of drunkenness, (confess anytime you have been drunk), and renounce... I am not a drunkard.

I repent of rivalries, (confess any rivalries), I am not one who partakes in rivalry.

MORE SCRIPTURES FOR REPENTANCE AND RENOUNCING SINS

Below are Here are mores scriptures To Use For repenting And renouncing Sin: you must have moments of introspection and self-examination to bring further conviction of sin. After reading the following scriptures ask the Lord to show you if there is anything else you need to repent of before going into battle. then repent of them and renounce them in prayer!

This is what I pray, "Dear Heavenly Father, search my heart and see if there is anything wicked in me. Lead me to repentance and to the way everlasting."

Romans 3:23 KJV
"For all have sinned, and come short of the glory of God;"

Mark 7:21-22 KJV
21 For from within, out of the heart of men, proceed evil thoughts, adulteries, fornications, murders,

James 4:17 KJV

17 Therefore to him that knoweth to do good, and doeth it not, to him it is sin.

Isaiah 59:1-15 King James Version (KJV)

1 Behold, the Lord's hand is not shortened, that it cannot save; neither his ear heavy, that it cannot hear:

2 But your iniquities have separated between you and your God, and your sins have hid his face from you, that he will not hear.

3 For your hands are defiled with blood, and your fingers with iniquity; your lips have spoken lies, your tongue hath muttered perverseness.

4 None calleth for justice, nor any pleadeth for truth: they trust in vanity, and speak lies; they conceive mischief, and bring forth iniquity.

5 They hatch cockatrice' eggs, and weave the spider's web: he that eateth of their eggs dieth, and that which is crushed breaketh out into a viper.

6 Their webs shall not become garments, neither shall they cover themselves with their works: their works are works of iniquity, and the act of violence is in their hands.

7 Their feet run to evil, and they make haste to shed innocent blood: their thoughts are thoughts of iniquity; wasting and destruction are in their paths.

8 The way of peace they know not; and there is no judgment in their goings: they have made them crooked paths: whosoever goeth therein shall not know peace.

9 Therefore is judgment far from us, neither doth justice overtake us: we wait for light, but behold obscurity; for brightness, but we walk in darkness.

10 We grope for the wall like the blind, and we grope as if we had no eyes: we stumble at noon day as in the night; we are in desolate places as dead men.

11 We roar all like bears, and mourn sore like doves: we look for judgment, but there is none; for salvation, but it is far off from us.

12 For our transgressions are multiplied before thee, and our sins testify against us: for our transgressions are with us; and as for our iniquities, we know them;

13 In transgressing and lying against the LORD, and departing away from our God, speaking oppression and revolt, conceiving and uttering from the heart words of falsehood.

14 And judgment is turned away backward, and justice standeth afar off: for truth is fallen in the street, and equity cannot enter.

15 Yea, truth faileth; and he that departeth from evil maketh himself a prey: and the LORD saw it, and it displeased him that there was no judgment.

Exodus 20:1-17 KJV
1 And God spake all these words, saying,

2 I am the LORD thy God, which have brought thee out of the land of Egypt, out of the house of bondage.

3 Thou shalt have no other gods before me.

4 Thou shalt not make unto thee any graven image, or any likeness of any thing that is in heaven above, or that is in the earth beneath, or that is in the water under the earth.

5 Thou shalt not bow down thyself to them, nor serve them: for I the LORD thy God am a jealous God, visiting the iniquity of the fathers upon the children unto the third and fourth generation of them that hate me;

6 And shewing mercy unto thousands of them that love me, and keep my commandments.

7 Thou shalt not take the name of the LORD thy God in vain; for the LORD will not hold him guiltless that taketh his name in vain.

8 Remember the sabbath day, to keep it holy.

9 Six days shalt thou labour, and do all thy work:

10 But the seventh day is the sabbath of the LORD thy God: in it thou shalt not do any work, thou, nor thy son, nor thy daughter, thy manservant, nor thy maidservant, nor thy cattle, nor thy stranger that is within thy gates:

11 For in six days the LORD made heaven and earth, the sea, and all that in them is, and rested the seventh day: wherefore the LORD blessed the sabbath day, and hallowed it.

12 Honour thy father and thy mother: that thy days may be long upon the land which the LORD thy God giveth thee.

13 Thou shalt not kill.

14 Thou shalt not commit adultery.

15 Thou shalt not steal.

16 Thou shalt not bear false witness against thy neighbour.

17 Thou shalt not covet thy neighbour's house, thou shalt not covet thy neighbour's wife, nor his manservant, nor his maidservant, nor his ox, nor his ass, nor any thing that is thy neighbour's.

Colossian 3:5-7 KJV
5 Mortify therefore your members which are upon the earth; fornication, uncleanness, inordinate affection, evil concupiscence, and covetousness, which is idolatry:

6 For which things' sake the wrath of God cometh on the children of disobedience:

7 In the which ye also walked some time, when ye lived in them.

2 Timothy 3:1-9 KJV
1 This know also, that in the last days perilous times shall come.

2 For men shall be lovers of their own selves, covetous, boasters, proud, blasphemers, disobedient to parents, unthankful, unholy,

3 Without natural affection, trucebreakers, false accusers, incontinent, fierce, despisers of those that are good,

4 Traitors, heady, highminded, lovers of pleasures more than lovers of God;

5 Having a form of godliness, but denying the power thereof: from such turn away.

6 For of this sort are they which creep into houses, and lead captive silly women laden with sins, led away with divers lusts,

7 Ever learning, and never able to come to the knowledge of the truth.

8 Now as Jannes and Jambres withstood Moses, so do these also resist the truth: men of corrupt minds, reprobate concerning the faith.

9 But they shall proceed no further: for their folly shall be manifest unto all men, as their's also was.

Next is blowing the Trumpet also known as the shofar, If you have one. If you do not, then prophetically blow a trumpet. Relook back to Numbers 10: 9, ""And if ye go to war in your land against the enemy that oppresseth you, then ye shall blow an alarm with the trumpets; and ye shall be remembered before the Lord your God, and ye shall be saved from your enemies." I have included three links to play on YouTube if you do not own a shofar.

Israelites would use the shofar to communicate to the community was going on. There are four sounds of the shofar. First sound is Tekiah which is a call to attention. Tekiah is a sound of a long blast. Second sound is the Shevarim which is a call to worship. It is three blasts in a row - ——, - ——, - ——,

The third sound is the Teruh, the Teruh is sound for battle. Teruh sound is short blasts in a row - - - - - . The fourth sound is Tekiah Gadolah which is a call or sound for peace. It is a long blast, you keep blowing it till you have no more breath. ————————.

Before we start our prayer, we want to blow the shofar and first use the sound of the Tekiah to get everyone's attention. Next we blow the shofar for the sound of worship, which is the Shevarim. After that we start the prayer with Judah.

After introducing Judah into the prayer then you want to blow the shofar using the Teruah sound, to announce war.

If you do not have a shofar, there are great YouTube videos out there.Before we start our prayer, we want to blow the shofar and first use the sound of the Tekiah to get everyone's attention. Next we blow the shofar for the sound of worship, which is the Shevarim. After that we start the prayer with Judah.

Tekiah is a call for attention

https://youtu.be/CJr9t7YJ4uQ

Teruah is the war of alarm.

https://youtu.be/zrw-_ZJCYTs

Shevarim is a call to worship.

https://youtu.be/-dp2Vh5Ljc8

Instructions: Put pen and paper next to you when you first start praying because the Holy Spirit may show you what specific blessing to pray for you and specialize it for you. Then you may have to repeat the pray the way the Holy Spirit shows you.

Now you are Ready to begin the main prayer, Going, into battle to get back what the enemy has stolen down or bloodlines.

Dear heavenly Father, we come to glorify and to honor you. We praise your holy name. We thank you for all the greatness you have done in the past. And we thank you for the present and future testimonies. Your word says that we overcome the enemy by the blood of the Lamb and the word of our testimonies. There is none like you, and we worship you. We thank you for your Son, Jesus Christ, who died on the cross for us so we can be reconciled back to you. Lord Holy Spirit, we ask for your presence and manifestation. By Jesus, we are able to approach the throne of grace by Jesus's shed blood. We go into spiritual battle to receive back everything the enemy has stolen from both sides of our bloodline.

Romans 2:11 AMPC
11 For God shows no partiality [undue favor or unfairness; with Him one man is not different from another].

Hebrews 4:16 KJV
16 Let us therefore come boldly unto the throne of grace, that we may obtain mercy, and find grace to help in time of need.

We thank you that you are no respecter of persons. What you will do for one, you will do for all, so we are able to approach the throne of grace through Jesus as we go into battle.

We position ourselves with the tribe of Judah to get back what the enemy has stolen down our bloodline from our mothers' side and fathers' side, for Judah's name means praise. As we join with him in praising you and giving you all the glory and honor due to you.

(Praying Genesis 49:8 - 10)
8 Judah, thou art he whom thy brethren shall praise: thy hand shall be in the neck of thine enemies; thy father's children shall bow down before thee.
9 Judah is a lion's whelp: from the prey, my son, thou art gone up: he stooped down, he couched as a lion, and as an old lion; who shall rouse him up?
10 The sceptre shall not depart from Judah, nor a lawgiver from between his feet, until Shiloh come; and unto him shall the gathering of the people be

Judah's hand shall be in the neck of the enemy, and his father's children shall bow down before him. Because of this, we take hold of our enemies' necks and decree that our enemies will bow down before us.

"Judah is a lion's welp: Thou art gone up: "We are as the lions that devoured our enemies as prey… "He stooped down, he crouched as a lion, and as an old lion; who shall rouse him up?" And as a lion that crouches low, and as a lioness who is about to pounce on her prey, we crouch down none will stop us.

"The scepter shall not depart from him, Nor a lawgiver from between his feet, until Shiloh comes; and unto Him shall gathering of the people be.

We stand in authority with the ruler's scepter, and we take back our authority and power for our descendants who shall bear the ruler's scepter for times to come.

(Praying through Deuteronomy 33:7)
7 And this is the blessing of Judah: and he said, Hear, Lord, the voice of Judah, and bring him unto his people: let his hands be sufficient for him; and be thou an help to him from his enemies.

Hear please, Lord, the cry of Judah; and as we stand with the tribe of Judah, bring to us our people with our own hands as we defend our cause. Oh, be our help against our foes. Thank you, Jesus for the tribe of Judah and its help.

Everything that was taken from us, we reclaim it all now as we continue in battle. And we position ourselves with the tribe of Issachar to help us through the generations of our bloodline. His name means reward, and we call for our reward as we stand with Issachar. We ask you, Father Lord God, for the understanding of what we should do to reclaim our reward as we stand with the tribe of Issachar. The tribe of Issachar understands the times and what Israel ought to do (1 Chronicles 12:32). "**32** And of the children of Issachar, which were men that had understanding of the times, to know what Israel ought to do; the heads of them were two hundred; and all their brethren were at their commandment."

We thank you, Father, for the tribe of Issachar helping us to have perfect timing in this battle.

(Pray through Genesis 49:14-15)
14 Issachar is a strong ass couching down between two burdens:15 And he saw that rest was good, and the land that it was pleasant; and bowed his shoulder to bear, and became a servant unto tribute.

We take back land, inheritances, dividends, relationships, and all treasures that were stolen from our bloodline down both sides, and we rest in the Lord.

(Pray through Deuteronomy 33:18-19)
18 And of Zebulun he said, Rejoice, Zebulun, in thy going out; and, Issachar, in thy tents.

19 They shall call the people unto the mountain; there they shall offer sacrifices of righteousness: for they shall suck of the abundance of the seas, and of treasures hid in the sand.

May we rejoice in our properties and homes, for we shall suck of the abundance of the sea and treasures hidden in the sand, in Jesus's name. We receive the blessings of Issachar. Thank you, Jesus.

We position ourselves with the tribe of Zebulun and because his name means a gift, dowery, and dwell. May we receive the blessings, gifts, dowery, and dwellings of the tribe of Zebulun.

(Pray through Genesis 49:13)
13 Zebulun shall dwell at the haven of the sea; and he shall be for an haven of ships; and his border shall be unto Zidon.

(Pray again Deuteronomy 33:18 -19)
18 And of Zebulun he said, Rejoice, Zebulun, in thy going out; and, Issachar, in thy tents. **19** They shall call the people unto the mountain; there they shall offer sacrifices of righteousness: for they shall suck of the abundance of the seas, and of treasures hid in the sand

We feast on Zebulun's and Issachar's abundance of the sea and the treasures hidden in the sand. We pray and receive Zebulun in joining us in battle in Jesus's mighty name.

Now we take a position with the tribe of Gad to join us in the spiritual warfare to receive back everything that the enemy has stolen from our bloodlines, on both sides. Gad means fortune. Lord make us fortunate as Gad's name meaning. We thank you, Jesus.

(Praying through Genesis 49:19)
19 Gad, a troop shall overcome him: but he shall overcome at the last. Lord make and enlarge our numbers in battle as a troop and crush our enemies at last. Thank you, Jesus, for Gad will help us to overcome at last.

(Praying through Deuteronomy 33:20-21)
20 And of Gad he said, Blessed be he that enlargeth Gad: he dwelleth as a lion, and teareth the arm with the crown of the head.

21 And he provided the first part for himself, because there, in a portion of the lawgiver, was he seated; and he came with the heads of the people, he executed the justice of the Lord, and his judgments with Israel.

Thank you, Father, for Gad joining us. Give us a crown for our heads as you did Gad and empower us to tear our enemies like a lion with it. Gad helps to bring forth justice and judgment on our behalf.

Thank you, Jesus.

We position ourselves with the tribe of Ephraim for battle. Ephraim was born in the seventh month, which means completion. We decree that this prayer is brought to completion and that we are fruitful, for Ephraim's name means fruitful. Lord Jesus make us the strength of our Father's head just as Ephraim is the strength of his father's head,

(Psalm 60:7) "**7** Gilead is mine, and Manasseh is mine; Ephraim also is the strength of mine head; Judah is my lawgiver;" We thank you for Ephraim to help us in battle.

(Pray through Genesis 48:19 -20)
"... his seed shall become a multitude of nations. ...In thee shall Israel bless, saying, God make thee as Ephraim and as Manasseh: and he set Ephraim before Manasseh."

We thank you, Jesus, for being our God who restores. Whatever seed Satan has stolen, such as miscarriage or untimely death or even permanent and sickly children, we ask for restoration of it all now in this time in Jesus's name amen.

(Pray through Deuteronomy 33: 13 -17)
13 And of Joseph he said, Blessed of the Lord be his land, for the precious things of heaven, for the dew, and for the deep that coucheth beneath,

14 And for the precious fruits brought forth by the sun, and for the precious things put forth by the moon,

15 And for the chief things of the ancient mountains, and for the precious things of the lasting hills,

16 And for the precious things of the earth and fulness thereof, and for the good will of him that dwelt in the bush: let the blessing come upon the head of Joseph, and upon the top of the head of him that was separated from his brethren.

17 His glory is like the firstling of his bullock, and his horns are like the horns of unicorns: with them he shall push the people together to the ends of the earth: and they are the ten thousands of Ephraim, and they are the thousands of Manasseh.

Thank you for the blessings of Joseph that fell to Manasseh and Ephraim. Lord, please bless our land with the precious things of heaven, and for the dew of heaven blessing.

Thank you, Jesus.

We position ourselves with Manasseh for battle. Manasseh was born in the eighth month; eight is the number that symbolizes new beginnings; we thank you, Jesus, for a new beginning, a fresh start. Manasseh means for God has made me forget all my toil and all my father's house. Thank you, God, for we forget what lies behind us and move into new territory, to new beginnings, with the tribe of Manasseh. "and his horns are like the horns of unicorns:....," Please give us the strength of the unicorn against our adversaries. May we also have the ability and influence to "push the people together to the ends of the earth:...", And according to Deuteronomy 33:17, they are the thousands of Manasseh.

We position ourselves with Benjamin for battle, to get back everything that the enemy has stolen from our ancestors, us, and our bloodline on each side. Benjamin meaning son of the right hand. We ask for the son of the right hand to battle with us.

(Pray through Genesis 49:27)
27 Benjamin shall ravin as a wolf: in the morning he shall devour the prey, and at night he shall divide the spoil.

Thank you, Jesus, for the tribe of Benjamin who will help us shred our enemies, devour the prey, and divide the spoil. Thank you, Lord. Benjamin was the only one born in the promised land. We thank you, Jesus, as we move into our promised land.

(Pray through Deuteronomy 33:12)
12 And of Benjamin he said, The beloved of the Lord shall dwell in safety by him; and the Lord shall cover him all the day long, and he shall dwell between his shoulders.

Thank you, Lord, that you have made us your beloved and cause us to dwell in safety by You. Cover us, Lord, all day long, especially in this battle. May we dwell between your shoulders.

Thank you, Jesus.

We position ourselves with the tribe of Dan for the battle to reclaim everything the enemy has stolen down our bloodline, on each side. We thank you, Jesus, for Dan means judge, and we thank you that our case will be judged righteously and in our favor. According to:

Genesis 49:16-18
16 Dan shall judge his people, as one of the tribes of Israel.

17 Dan shall be a serpent by the way, an adder in the path, that biteth the horse heels, so that his rider shall fall backward.

18 I have waited for thy salvation, O Lord.

Let us be as the serpent, by the way. And an adder in the path of our enemies that have taken our precious possessions.

We bite the horses' heels with Dan, so that enemy riders fall backward and we take back our precious possessions now in the mighty name of Jesus.

(Pray through Deuteronomy 33:22)
22 And of Dan he said, Dan is a lion's whelp: he shall leap from Bashan. Bashan represents the enemies of Christ, and we thank you, Jesus, for the tribe of Dan. We leap with Dan from Bashan, in help retrieving the spoil of the enemy, in Jesus's name.

We position ourselves with the tribe of Asher for battle. For Asher means happy, blessed. Thank you, Lord God, for this, is a time of happiness by all your blessings that you have given us. Thank you for all the restored blessings in Jesus's name.

(Pray through Genesis 49:20)
20 Out of Asher, his bread shall be fat, and he shall yield royal dainties.

Thank you, Jesus; we receive the bread that is fat and royal dainties.

(Pray through Deuteronomy 33:24)
24 And of Asher he said, Let Asher be blessed with children; let him be acceptable to his brethren, and let him dip his foot in oil.

Father, we thank you for blessing us with children, grandchildren and continuing our lineage. We praise you because you have made us acceptable amongst our brethren.

We pray that all the oil (anointing) that was taken down our bloodline to do your work that it is replenished double the portion, in Jesus's mighty name amen.

We position ourselves with Naphtali for the battle and take back all that was stolen down our bloodline on our mother's side and father's side in the name of Jesus. Naphtali means my struggle. Our lineage has had strife and has struggled for a lot has been stolen. But our struggle has ended in the name of Jesus.

(Pray Genesis 49:21)
21 Naphtali is a hind let loose: he giveth goodly words.

We give goodly words with Naphtali as we give our God of Abraham, Isaac, and Jacob praise and worship for this mighty power of God to restore all that was stolen down our bloodline to us now in Jesus's name.

(Pray through Deuteronomy 33:23)
23 And of Naphtali he said, O Naphtali, satisfied with favour, and full with the blessing of the Lord: possess thou the west and the south.

Thank you, Jesus, for your favor and blessings, and thank you for we possess our new inheritance in the mighty name of Jesus amen. We give you all the glory, praise, and thanks to your name in Jesus's name, amen, and amen. Thanks be to God and Jesus name amen. We praise and worship you in the mighty name of Jesus, amen and amen and amen.

References

Double Portion Section

https://www.chabad.org/library/article_cdo/aid/3922260/jewish/About-the-Month-of-Nisan.htm

Judah

Wikipedia contributors, "Nisan," *Wikipedia, The Free Encyclopedia,* https://en.wikipedia.org/w/index.php?title=Nisan&oldid=984824269 (accessed November 21, 2020).

http://mycoffeechurch.com/the-name-judah-is-a-hebrew-word-meaning-worship/

Issachar

https://www.hebrew4christians.com/Holidays/Rosh_Chodesh/Iyyar/iyyar.html

https://bje.org.au/knowledge-centre/jewish-calendar/the-month-of-iyar/

http://www.israelnationalnews.com/Articles/Article.aspx/25599

https://biblehub.com/1_chronicles/12-33.htm

https://en.m.wikipedia.org/wiki/Issachar

https://biblehub.com/hebrew/3485.htm

https://biblehub.com/genesis/49-14.htm

Zebulun

https://www.google.com/search?q=zebulun+name+meaning&ie=UTF-8&oe=UTF-8&hl=en-us&client=safari

https://www.biblestudytools.com/dictionary/zebulun/

https://biblehub.com/1_chronicles/12-33.htm

Commentary Ellicott's Commentary for English Readers Judges 5:14

"Deuteronomy 33:18-19 - About Zebulun he said: "Rejoice ...." https://www.biblestudytools.com/deuteronomy/passage/?q=deuteronomy+33:18-19.

https://www.biblestudytools.com/judges/5-18.html

https://www.biblestudytools.com/1-chronicles/12-40.html

Reuben

https://www.google.com/search?q=What+does+the+name+Ruben+mean+in+Hebrew&ie=UTF-8&oe=UTF-8&hl=en-us&client=safari

Simeon

2020. *Behind the Name*. May 29. Accessed December 1, 2020. https://www.behindthename.com/name/ephraim.
Benner, Jeff A. n.d. *https://ancient-hebrew.org/*. Accessed 12 4, 2020. https://ancient-hebrew.org/names/Simeon.htm.

(Benner 1999, https://ancient-hebrew.org/)

https://www.ancient-hebrew.org/names/Simeon.htm

https://biblehub.com/1_chronicles/12-25.htm

Gad

https://www.google.com/search?q=meaning+of+the+bane+Gad&ie=UTF-8&oe=UTF-8&hl=en-us&client=safari

https://biblehub.com/1_chronicles/12-37.htm

Ephraim

2020. Behind the Name. May 29. Accessed December 1, 2020. https://www.behindthename.com/name/ephraim.